From our Kitchen to Yours

ALL-TIME-FAVORITE RECIPES
From

Washington
COOKS

Dedication

For every cook who wants to create amazing
recipes from the great cooks of
Washington state.

Appreciation

Thanks to all our Washington state cooks who shared
their delightful and delicious recipes with us!

Gooseberry Patch
An imprint of Globe Pequot
246 Goose Lane
Guilford, CT 06437
www.gooseberrypatch.com
1 800 854 6673

Copyright 2019, Gooseberry Patch
978-162093-343-5

Do you have a tried & true recipe... tip, craft or
memory that you'd like to see featured in a
Gooseberry Patch cookbook? Visit our website at
www.gooseberrypatch.com and follow the easy steps
to submit your favorite family recipe.

Or send them to us at:

Gooseberry Patch
PO Box 812
Columbus, OH 43216-0812

Don't forget to include the number of servings your
recipe makes, plus your name, address, phone
number and email address. If we select your recipe,
your name will appear right along with it... and you'll
receive a FREE copy of the book!

Washington
COOKS

EATING IN THE EVERGREEN STATE

Washington state, lush with scenic ocean and mountain views, offers a dining paradise. Seafood lovers can delight in various kinds of trout, whitefish, sturgeon, cod, halibut, flounder, crab and, of course, salmon.

Farmers raise winter and spring wheat, along with hops for making beer. Other crops include potatoes, asparagus, peas, dry beans, sweet corn and hay. Long known as the king of apples, such as Red or Golden Delicious, newer varieties like Cameo and Honey Crisp now are harvested, too. Plums, prunes, apricots, blueberries and cherries are grown in abundance, along with numerous grapes and berry crops. . .cranberries, raspberries and strawberries. And of course, you can always find a good cup of coffee!

In this Gooseberry Patch cookbook, the talented cooks from the Evergreen State share their recipes that are dear to their hearts. You'll find everything from Apple Pie Bread and Cranberry Scones to Ginger-Lime Grilled Salmon and Famous Blueberry Cake. We know you will love this collection of tried & true recipes from these amazing cooks from beautiful Washington state.

OUR STORY

Back in 1984, our families were neighbors in little Delaware, Ohio. With small children, we wanted to do what we loved and stay home with the kids too. We had always shared a love of home cooking and so, **Gooseberry Patch** was born.

Almost immediately, we found a connection with our customers and it wasn't long before these friends started sharing recipes. Since then we've enjoyed publishing hundreds of cookbooks with your tried & true recipes.

We know we couldn't have done it without our friends all across the country and we look forward to continuing to build a community with you. Welcome to the **Gooseberry Patch** family!

JoAnn & Vickie

TABLE OF CONTENTS

CHAPTER ONE

GOOD-START

Breakfast & Brunch

WHETHER YOU ARE UP FOR CLIMBING A MOUNTAIN, GOING TO THE FARMERS' MARKET OR RELAXING AT THE BEACH, THESE BREAKFAST & BRUNCH RECIPES WILL START YOUR DAY RIGHT.

APPLE PIE BREAD

**MACKENNA ASK
LYNNWOOD, WA**

We especially enjoy this bread at autumn apple-picking time, but it's wonderful year 'round! It freezes well too.

3 c. all-purpose flour
1 t. baking powder
1 t. baking soda
1 t. salt
2 t. cinnamon
1 t. nutmeg
1/2 t. ground cloves
3 eggs, beaten
1 c. oil
1-1/4 c. brown sugar, packed
1 c. sugar
1 T. vanilla extract
2 c. Fuji apples, peeled, cored and diced
3/4 c. chopped pecans

1 Sift flour, baking powder, baking soda, salt and spices together in a bowl; set aside. Beat eggs, oil, sugars and vanilla together in a separate large bowl. Add flour mixture to egg mixture; beat well. Add apples and pecans; stir until mixed well.

2 Pour batter into 2 greased 8"x4" loaf pans. Bake at 325 degrees for 40 to 60 minutes, until a tester inserted in the center comes out clean. Cool pans on a wire rack for 20 minutes. Turn bread out of pans; cool completely.

Makes 2 loaves

PENNSYLVANIA DUTCH POTATO PANCAKES

**JO ANN
GOOSEBERRY PATCH**

Crisp and golden, these potato pancakes are perfect with breakfast sausage and eggs over easy. Add a dollop of sour cream...yum!

2 lbs. potatoes, peeled and quartered
2 onions, quartered
1 egg
1-1/2 c. all-purpose flour
2 t. baking powder
1 t. lemon juice
1/8 t. nutmeg
1 T. salt
pepper to taste
oil for frying

1 Put potatoes and onions through a food grinder, using a fine blade. May also be grated using a hand grater. Combine potatoes and onions in a colander; drain thoroughly and transfer to a large bowl. Add remaining ingredients except oil; mix well. Add 1/4 inch oil to a heavy skillet; heat to about 375 degrees. Drop potato mixture by tablespoonfuls into hot oil. Cook for about 10 minutes, or until golden on both sides. Drain on paper towels; serve warm.

Makes 6 servings

ANGEL HAIR BRUNCH FRITTATA

VICKIE
GOOSEBERRY PATCH

Whenever my friends come for brunch, this dish is a must! Very easy to make and you can vary it with veggies and cheeses you have on hand. To double for a potluck, use a 13"x9" baking pan.

1 Cook pasta according to package directions; drain. Meanwhile, in a bowl, whisk together eggs, milk, Parmesan cheese, salt and pepper; mix well. Add cooked pasta to egg mixture; mix gently and spread in a lightly greased 9" pie plate. Top with provolone cheese and vegetables. Cover with aluminum foil.

2 Bake at 350 degrees for 20 minutes. Uncover; bake 15 minutes longer. Cut into wedges and serve warm, topped with pasta sauce.

Makes 6 servings

8-oz. pkg. angel hair pasta, uncooked

3 eggs, lightly beaten

1/4 c. milk

1/2 c. grated Parmesan cheese

1/2 t. salt

1/8 t. pepper

3/4 c. provolone cheese, shredded

1/2 c. asparagus, chopped

1/2 c. tomato, chopped

1/2 c. sliced black olives, drained

Garnish: tomato and garlic pasta sauce, warmed

MRS. L'S BUTTERMILK BISCUITS

MICHELLE LOCKETT
LEBAM, WA

My sister-in-law always makes these biscuits for holiday dinners. They go quickly, especially with her homemade jam & jelly.

1 In a large bowl, sift together flour, baking powder, baking soda and salt. Cut in shortening with a pastry blender to a mealy consistency. Add buttermilk; stir until blended.

2 Turn out dough onto a floured surface. Knead 18 times; pat out 3/4-inch thick. Cut biscuits with a biscuit cutter; place on a lightly greased baking sheet. Bake at 450 degrees for 12 minutes.

Makes one to 2 dozen biscuits

2 c. all-purpose flour

1 T. baking powder

1/4 t. baking soda

1/2 t. salt

5 T. shortening

1 c. buttermilk

BANANA-NUT BREAD

CAROLYN AYERS
KENT, WA

This scrumptious recipe has been in my family for about seventy-five years. My grandmother lived in Bermuda and made this bread using bananas picked from the banana trees in her yard.

2 c. all-purpose flour
1 c. sugar
1 t. baking soda
1/4 t. salt
1/2 c. canola or safflower oil
2 eggs, beaten
3 very ripe bananas, mashed
1 c. chopped walnuts or pecans

1 Combine flour, sugar, baking soda and salt in a bowl; mix well and set aside. In a separate large bowl, mix oil and eggs; add bananas. Add flour mixture and mix well; stir in nuts.

2 Pour batter into a greased 9"x5" loaf pan or two, 7"x3" loaf pans. Bake at 350 degrees, 45 minutes for a regular loaf pan or 25 to 30 minutes for 2 smaller pans.

Makes one regular loaf or 2 smaller loaves

FARMSTYLE BACON & EGG GRAVY

LISA KASTNING
MARYSVILLE, WA

This recipe is fresh-from-the-farm delicious and so easy to make! It's a terrific way to use up some hard-boiled eggs too.

6 slices bacon, diced
5 T. all-purpose flour
1-1/2 c. water
12-oz. can evaporated milk
3 eggs, hard-boiled, peeled and sliced or chopped
salt and pepper to taste
Optional: cider vinegar to taste
4 slices bread, toasted

1 In a skillet over medium heat, cook bacon until crisp. Remove bacon to paper towels and drain, reserving drippings in skillet. Add flour to drippings and whisk until blended. Cook over medium heat until golden, stirring constantly. Gradually add water and evaporated milk; continue stirring. Bring to a boil; cook and stir for 2 minutes, or until thickened.

2 Add bacon, eggs, salt, pepper and a sprinkle of vinegar, if desired. Serve spooned over toast slices.

Serves 2 to 4

TEN-GRAIN PANCAKES

ELLIE BARTON
COLVILLE, WA

We love these pancakes. When we camp at our cabin at the lake, we mix up the batter the night before.

1 Pour boiling water over cereal and cornmeal in a large bowl; stir until thickened. Add molasses; stir until cooled. Beat in buttermilk and eggs; set aside. In a separate bowl, combine flours, baking powder, baking soda and salt. Stir in cereal mixture and butter or oil until well mixed; don't overmix.

2 Cover and refrigerate if making batter ahead of time. Drop batter by 1/4 to 1/3 cupfuls onto a lightly greased hot griddle. Cook until golden on both sides.

Serves 6

2 c. boiling water
1 c. 10-grain cereal
1/2 c. cornmeal
2 T. molasses, or more to taste
2 c. buttermilk
5 eggs, beaten
2 c. whole-wheat flour
1 c. all-purpose flour
2 T. baking powder
1/2 t. baking soda
1 T. salt
1/3 c. melted butter or canola oil

KITCHEN TIP

Frying up a skillet of bacon for breakfast? If there's no spatter guard handy, a large sieve can do the job. Just place it face-down over the skillet.

OVERNIGHT APPLE-CINNAMON OATS

DANA ROWAN
SPOKANE, WA

I was looking for a healthy, filling breakfast that I wouldn't have to fuss with early in the morning. This slow-cooker recipe is always a hit with the family. It's so nice to wake up to a warm breakfast!

2 apples, peeled, cored and chopped

2 c. milk

1-1/2 c. water

1/2 c. unsweetened applesauce

1 c. steel-cut oats, uncooked

3 T. brown sugar, packed

1 T. butter, diced

1 t. cinnamon

1/4 t. salt

Garnish: maple syrup, milk, applesauce, chopped walnuts

1 Spray a slow cooker with non-stick vegetable spray. Add all ingredients except garnish; stir.

2 Cover and cook on low setting for about 7 hours. If desired, stir in a little more milk or water to thin to desired consistency. Spoon into bowls; garnish as desired.

Makes 8 servings

JENNIFER'S BBQ SCRAMBLED EGGS

JENNIFER ROSE BLAY
PUYALLUP, WA

My Dad taught me to put barbecue sauce in scrambled eggs as a special treat. Along with the herbs and spices, the sauce gives these eggs a wonderful flavor. I hope you and your family enjoy this recipe as much as my husband and I do!

1 In a large bowl, whisk together eggs, half-and-half, barbecue sauce and seasonings; set aside.

2 Melt butter in a large skillet over medium heat; pour egg mixture into skillet. Scramble eggs over medium-low to medium heat to desired consistency. If desired, sprinkle with shredded cheese just before serving.

Makes 4 servings

8 eggs, beaten
1/4 c. half-and-half
4 t. hickory barbecue sauce
1 t. dried parsley
1/2 t. dried basil
1/2 t. garlic powder
1/2 t. onion powder
1/2 t. celery salt
1/4 t. salt
1/4 t. pepper, or to taste
1/8 t. cayenne pepper
1 T. butter
Optional: shredded Cheddar cheese

BONUS IDEA

If you like to use a lot of herbs, start an indoor herb garden so you will have them handy for those special recipes.

BOWL-FREE CEREAL-TO-GO

AMANDA PENNINGS
WALLA WALLA, WA

Cereal without the milk! A big handful of this and I'm out the door, ready to start my day.

1/4 c. sugar
1/2 t. cinnamon
1 c. bite-size crispy corn cereal squares
1 c. bite-size crispy rice cereal squares
1 c. bite-size crispy wheat cereal squares
1 c. honey-nut doughnut-shaped oat cereal
3/4 c. sliced almonds, toasted
1/3 c. butter, melted
1 c. dried banana chips
1/2 c. dried blueberries or raisins

1 In a small bowl, mix sugar and cinnamon; set aside. In a large, microwave-safe bowl, combine cereals and melted butter; toss until evenly coated. Microwave, uncovered, on high for 2 minutes, stirring after one minute. Stir in sugar mixture and banana chips until evenly coated.

2 Microwave, uncovered, for one additional minute. Spread on wax paper to cool. Transfer to an airtight container; stir in blueberries or raisins.

Makes 12 to 14 servings

MELT-IN-YOUR-MOUTH BISCUITS

SHERRI HAGEL
SPOKANE, WA

Split and served with butter and jam or topped with sausage gravy, these flaky biscuits live up to their name!

1-1/2 c. all-purpose flour
1/2 c. whole-wheat flour
4 t. baking powder
1/2 t. salt
2 T. sugar
1/4 c. chilled butter, sliced
1/4 c. shortening
2/3 c. milk
1 egg, beaten

1 In a large bowl, sift flours, baking powder, salt and sugar together; cut in butter and shortening. Add milk; stir in egg. Knead on a floured surface until smooth; roll out to 1/2-inch thickness. Cut with a biscuit cutter; place biscuits on ungreased baking sheets. Bake at 450 degrees for 10 to 15 minutes, until golden.

Makes one to 2 dozen

BUTTERSCOTCH GRANOLA

ALICIA SAUVAGEAU
EAST WENATCHEE, WA

This is the best granola I have ever eaten. My kids and husband love it over berry yogurt!

1 Mix together all ingredients except butterscotch chips in a deep, greased 13"x9" baking pan or a roaster pan.

2 Bake at 300 degrees for 40 minutes, stirring every 10 minutes. Add butterscotch chips during the last 5 minutes; mix well after melted to distribute evenly. Cool. Store in an airtight container.

Makes 5 quarts

10 c. long-cooking oats, uncooked
2 sleeves graham crackers, crushed
2 c. sweetened flaked coconut
1 c. pecans, finely chopped
3/4 c. brown sugar, packed
1 t. baking soda
1 t. salt
2 c. butter, melted
16-oz. pkg. butterscotch chips

GOLDENROD EGGS

FAWN MCKENZIE
WENATCHEE, WA

This simple dish will become a favorite comfort food as well as a great weeknight brunch.

1 Place egg yolks in a small bowl; mash and set aside. Chop whites and set aside. Heat butter or drippings in a medium saucepan over medium high heat; whisk in flour. Slowly pour in milk until desired consistency is achieved. Continue to heat through until mixture thickens. Stir in egg whites; season with salt and pepper as desired.

2 Spoon over toast or biscuits. Sprinkle mashed egg yolks over each serving.

Serves 4

5 to 6 eggs, hard-boiled, peeled and halved
6 T. butter or sausage drippings
6 T. all-purpose flour
2-3/4 c. to 3 c. milk
salt and pepper to taste
toast or split biscuits

CRANBERRY SCONES

CATHY LIGHT
SEDRO WOOLLEY, WA

I've had this recipe for so many years, it's a breakfast "must-have!"

2-1/2 c. all-purpose flour
2-1/2 t. baking powder
1/2 t. baking soda
3/4 c. butter, sliced
1 c. cranberries, chopped
2/3 c. sugar
3/4 c. buttermilk

1 Mix flour, baking powder and baking soda together in a large mixing bowl; cut in butter until mixture resembles coarse crumbs. Stir in cranberries and sugar; add buttermilk, mixing until just blended.

2 Divide dough in half; roll each portion into an 8-inch circle, about 1/2-inch thick, on a lightly floured surface. Cut each portion into 8 wedges; arrange wedges on ungreased baking sheets. Bake at 400 degrees for 12 to 15 minutes; remove to a wire rack to cool. Drizzle glaze over the tops.

Makes 16 servings

GLAZE:
2/3 c. powdered sugar
1 T. warm water
1/4 t. vanilla extract

1 Combine ingredients; mix well, adding additional warm water until desired spreading consistency is achieved.

CRANBERRY-NUT COFFEE CAKE

TINA HENGEN
CLARKSTON, WA

I bake this make-ahead coffee cake every Thanksgiving and Christmas Eve. My family really looks forward to this treat. In the morning it's easy to just pop it into the oven, bake and serve warm. It makes a yummy cake even without the cranberries, if you prefer.

1 In a bowl, stir together flour, baking powder, baking soda, salt and cinnamon; set aside. In a separate large bowl, blend together butter and sugars; add eggs, one at a time. Add buttermilk and flour mixture alternately to butter mixture, stirring well. Mix in cranberries, if using.

2 Spread batter evenly in a greased 13"x9" baking pan; sprinkle with Streusel Topping. Cover and refrigerate 8 hours to overnight. In the morning, bake at 350 degrees for about 45 minutes, or until a toothpick inserted in the center comes out clean. Cut into squares.

Serves 12

2 c. all-purpose flour
1 t. baking powder
1 t. baking soda
1/2 t. salt
1 t. cinnamon
1 c. butter
1 c. sugar
1/2 c. brown sugar, packed
2 eggs
1 c. Bulgarian or regular buttermilk
Optional: 1 c. sweetened dried cranberries

1 Stir ingredients together in a small bowl.

STREUSEL TOPPING:
1/2 c. brown sugar, packed
1/2 c. chopped pecans
1 t. cinnamon
1/4 t. nutmeg

CRESCENT QUICKIES

JODI BAKER
CHEHALIS, WA

This is a quick & easy way to "fancy-up" basic crescent rolls and make a tasty treat. Kids love them!

8-oz. tube refrigerated crescent rolls

1/2 c. favorite-flavor jam or preserves, divided

1 Divide rolls into 8 triangles; place flat on an ungreased baking sheet. Spread one tablespoon jam or preserves on each triangle. Roll into crescents; bake at 375 degrees for 11 to 13 minutes, until golden.

Makes 8

CRUSTLESS SOUTHWESTERN QUICHE

CINDE SHIELDS
ISSAQUAH, WA

Quiche is always a winner at my house...you can add just about anything you like with delicious results! This warm, satisfying quiche makes the most of your harvest. If you have garden-fresh corn and vine-ripened tomatoes on hand, by all means use them.

4 eggs, beaten

1 c. milk

1/4 c. fresh cilantro, chopped

1/2 t. chili powder

1/4 t. salt

1/4 t. pepper

1 c. frozen corn, thawed

1 tomato, chopped

1-1/4 c. shredded sharp Cheddar cheese

1/4 c. crumbled Cotija cheese or shredded Parmesan cheese

1 Spray a 9" glass pie plate with non-stick cooking spray. In a bowl, combine eggs, milk and seasonings; stir until blended. Stir in corn, tomato and cheeses; pour into pie plate.

2 Bake at 350 degrees for 40 to 50 minutes, until a knife tip inserted in the center comes out clean. Let stand 10 minutes; cut into wedges.

Serves 6

DENVER SCRAMBLE

KATHLEEN KENNEDY
RENTON, WA

All my menfolk love this dish! The recipe can easily be divided or multiplied depending on how many hungry diners you have. Add fresh fruit and buttered toast for a well-rounded meal.

1 Melt butter in a large skillet over medium heat until it starts to sizzle. Add ham, peppers and onion to skillet; cook until vegetables are crisp-tender. Meanwhile, whisk together eggs and milk in a bowl. Stir egg mixture into mixture in skillet; season with pepper. Reduce heat to medium-low. Cook until eggs are set, stirring occasionally, 4 to 5 minutes.

2 Remove skillet from heat. Top with cheese; let stand for a minute, until cheese melts. Sprinkle with tomatoes, if desired.

Serves 4 to 6

3 to 4 T. butter
1 lb. thick-sliced cooked deli ham, diced
1 c. green or red peppers, diced
1 c. yellow onion, diced
6 eggs
1/4 c. milk
pepper to taste
1/2 c. shredded Cheddar cheese
Optional: diced tomatoes

PARMESAN-GARLIC BISCUITS

JO ANN
GOOSEBERRY PATCH

These upside-down biscuits are a hit with any Italian dish!

1 Coat the bottom of a 9" pie plate with butter; sprinkle with celery seed and garlic. Cut each biscuit into quarters; arrange on top of butter mixture. Sprinkle with Parmesan cheese.

2 Bake at 425 degrees for 12 to 15 minutes. Invert onto a serving plate to serve.

Serves 8

3 T. butter, melted
1/4 t. celery seed
2 cloves garlic, minced
12-oz. tube refrigerated biscuits
2 T. grated Parmesan cheese

DOUBLE CHOCOLATE CHIP MUFFINS

VICKIE
GOOSEBERRY PATCH

So rich and chocolatey!

18-1/4 oz. pkg. chocolate
  fudge cake mix
3.9-oz. pkg. instant
  chocolate pudding mix
3/4 c. water
4 eggs beaten
1/2 c. oil
1/2 t. almond extract
6-oz. pkg. mini chocolate
  chips, frozen
Garnish: powdered
  sugar

1 Blend cake mix, pudding mix, water, eggs, oil and extract until smooth; fold in chocolate chips.

2 Fill greased muffin cups 3/4 full; bake at 350 degrees for 25 to 35 minutes. Cool; sprinkle with powdered sugar before serving.

Makes 2 dozen

HERBY BUBBLE BREAD

SUZY MCNEILLY
COLFAX, WA

This is a perfect bread to bring to a potluck or serve with soup. If you're looking for extra oomph, shake in some red pepper flakes!

3 1-lb. loaves frozen
  bread dough, thawed
  but still chilled
1/4 c. olive oil
3 T. Italian salad
  dressing mix
1 c. shredded sharp
  Cheddar cheese
1 t. garlic, minced
1 red onion, finely
  chopped

1 Cut dough into one-inch cubes; place in a large bowl. Spread remaining ingredients over top. Using your hands, toss until dough cubes are coated.

2 Place mixture in a greased 13"x9" baking pan. Place in a warm area; cover and let rise until double in size. Bake at 350 degrees for 20 to 25 minutes, until golden.

Serves 6 to 8

EARLY-RISER BREAKFAST

PATTY LAUGHERY
MOSES LAKE, WA

This has become a tradition at Easter and Christmas because it's so easy to prepare the night before and everyone loves it!

1 Arrange bread in an ungreased 13"x9" baking pan; sprinkle with cheeses and sausage. Set aside. Mix eggs and 2-1/2 cups milk together; pour over bread. Cover with aluminum foil; refrigerate overnight.

2 Combine remaining milk, soup and mustard; pour over bread mixture. Bake, uncovered, at 300 degrees for 1-1/2 hours.

Makes 8 servings

8 slices bread, cubed
1 c. shredded Cheddar cheese
1 c. shredded Monterey Jack cheese
1-1/2 lbs. ground pork sausage, browned and drained
4 eggs, beaten
3 c. milk, divided
10-3/4 oz. can cream of mushroom soup
3/4 t. dry mustard

MOMCY'S GRILLED FLATBREAD

LISA KASTNING
MARYSVILLE, WA

My mother-in-law's name is Nancy, but I have always called her "Momcy" as she's just like a second mom to me. She has given me many wonderful family-loved recipes. This is one of my favorites!

1 Heat water until very warm, about 110 to 115 degrees. Combine with yeast in a small bowl; let stand for 5 minutes. In a medium bowl, combine flour and salt. Add yeast mixture and one tablespoon olive oil to flour mixture. Stir to mix; knead until soft dough forms. Cover; let rise for 30 minutes.

2 Divide into 4 balls and roll into rounds, 1/8-inch thick. Lightly coat each side with remaining olive oil. Grill over medium-high heat until crisp and very lightly golden; sprinkle with coarse salt.

Makes 4 servings

1/2 c. warm water
1/2 t. active dry yeast
1-1/3 c. all-purpose flour
3/4 t. salt
2 T. olive oil, divided
coarse salt to taste

EGGS BENEDICT WITH SALMON

MELODY TAYNOR
EVERETT, WA

A scrumptious Pacific Northwest version of a breakfast favorite.

1-1/4 oz. pkg.
  Hollandaise sauce mix
chopped fresh dill to
  taste
4 t. white vinegar
6 eggs
3 English muffins, split
3 T. butter, softened
6 to 12 thin slices
  smoked salmon
Garnish: additional dill

1 Prepare sauce mix according to directions; add dill to taste and keep warm. To poach eggs, fill a skillet with 2 to 3 inches water. Add vinegar to water. Heat to boiling; reduce to a gentle simmer. Break eggs into a saucer, one at a time; carefully slip eggs into water. Cook 3 to 5 minutes, until whites and yolks are firm. Remove eggs with a slotted spoon.

2 Meanwhile, toast muffin halves and spread with butter. Top each muffin half with one to 2 slices salmon, a poached egg and a generous dollop of warm Hollandaise sauce. Sprinkle with dill.

Makes 3 to 6 servings

NANA'S WEDGE PANCAKES

PATRICIA O'KINS JOHNSON
SNOQUALMIE, WA

Years ago, my mother came up with this unique way of making pancakes so she could serve both of her grandkids at the same time!

2/3 c. all-purpose flour
2/3 c. whole-wheat flour
2/3 c. quick-cooking oats,
  uncooked
6 T. sugar, divided
4 t. baking powder
1/2 t. salt
2 eggs, beaten
2-1/3 c. milk
1/4 c. oil
1-1/2 t. cinnamon
3 to 4 T. butter, softened

1 In a bowl, combine flours, oats, 2 tablespoons sugar, baking powder and salt; set aside. In a large bowl, whisk together eggs, milk and oil. Add flour mixture to egg mixture; mix well. Batter will be thin. Let batter stand for 5 minutes. Combine cinnamon and remaining sugar in a cup. Lightly grease a griddle; heat until a water droplet sizzles on the surface.

2 Pour 1/2 cup batter onto griddle; spread to 7 or 8 inches in diameter. Cook until fairly dry on top. Turn and cook other side until lightly golden. When pancake is done, remove to a plate. Spread generously with a teaspoon of butter. Sprinkle with a teaspoon of cinnamon-sugar. As more pancakes are done, stack on top of previously cooked pancakes to make 8 layers. To serve, cut into wedges like a pie.

Serves 4

FAMILY FAVORITE BISCUITS

ELLIE BARTON
COLVILLE, WA

My family loves these biscuits! They are so simple and easy to make, so I can whip up a batch really quickly.

1 In a large bowl, mix flours, baking powder, baking soda and salt. Make a well in the center; set aside. In a measuring cup, combine beaten egg and enough milk to equal 2/3 cup. Stir in melted butter. Add egg mixture to the well in flour mixture. Stir just until combined; do not overmix.

2 Turn out dough onto a lightly floured surface. Knead dough 3 to 5 times, until smooth and uniform. Pat into a circle, 1/2-inch to 3/4-inch thick. Cut out dough with a biscuit cutter; place on a greased baking sheet. Biscuits should be just touching, not pressed together. Bake at 350 degrees for 10 to 12 minutes, until lightly golden and flaky.

Makes one dozen

1 c. all-purpose flour
1 c. whole-wheat flour
2 t. baking powder
1/2 t. baking soda
1/2 t. salt
1 egg, beaten
5 to 6 T. milk
1/3 c. butter, melted and
  cooled slightly

ITALIAN SCRAMBLE

KATHLEEN KENNEDY
RENTON, WA

My adaptation of a favorite restaurant's late-night offering. Use hot or mild sausage, or a combination of the two.

1 In a bowl, whisk together eggs and half-and-half or milk; set aside. Brown sausage in a large skillet over medium-high heat, breaking it up as it cooks; drain. Add egg mixture to sausage in skillet; reduce heat to medium-low.

2 Cook until eggs start to set. Add spinach and pepper. Cook, stirring occasionally, until eggs are set. Sprinkle with Parmesan cheese before serving.

Serves 4

8 eggs, beaten
1/4 c. half-and-half or
  milk
1 lb. Italian pork
  sausage links, casings
  removed
1/2 c. fresh spinach,
  chopped
pepper to taste
Garnish: shredded
  Parmesan cheese

CHAPTER TWO

SATISFYING

Soups, Salads & Sandwiches

EVEN IF IT IS RAINY OUTSIDE, YOU CAN COZY UP WITH A BOWL OF SOUL-SOOTHING SOUP, A SUNSHINY SALAD OR A TASTY SANDWICH FOR A LIGHT AND LIVELY LUNCH.

ALL-AMERICAN SANDWICHES

JO ANN
GOOSEBERRY PATCH

This is such a quick sandwich to make, but it is so hearty and filling! Switch out the blue cheese for a slice of Swiss if you prefer.

1-1/2 T. olive oil
1 red onion, thinly sliced
3-1/2 T. red wine
  vinegar
6 c. fresh arugula
  leaves, divided
1/4 c. mayonnaise
salt and pepper to taste
4 whole-grain ciabatta
  rolls, halved
3/4 lb. thinly sliced
  smoked deli turkey
1/4 c. crumbled blue
  cheese

1 Heat oil in a skillet over medium-high heat. Add onion and sauté until soft and lightly golden. Remove from heat and stir in vinegar. Set aside. Chop enough arugula to equal one cup. Stir in mayonnaise; season with salt and pepper.

2 Spread arugula mixture over cut sides of rolls. Divide turkey evenly among bottom halves of rolls. Top with cheese, onion mixture, remaining arugula leaves and top halves of rolls.

Serves 4

HOMEMADE APPLESAUCE

LISA NEECE
OLALLA, WA

Our family loves this tart-sweet applesauce in chilly weather.

6 Granny Smith apples,
  peeled, cored and sliced
1/2 c. sugar
cinnamon to taste

1 Place apples in a medium saucepan with just enough water to cover them; add sugar. Cook over medium-high heat for 10 to 15 minutes. Let cool; mash to desired consistency. Add cinnamon to taste.

Makes 4 servings

AMERICAN-STYLE PHO

CARLY ST. CLAIR
LYNNWOOD, WA

On a cold day, I made this soup for my son and myself. We loved it so much we just had to share it!

1 In a large saucepan, cook ramen noodles in water according to package instructions. Stir in seasoning packets; do not drain. Add chicken with juices; heat through.

2 To serve, divide onions and cabbage among 6 soup bowls; reserve some of each for garnish. Ladle soup into bowls. Garnish with reserved onions and cabbage.

Serves 6

3 3-oz. pkgs. chicken-flavored ramen noodles, uncooked

6 c. water

12-oz. can chicken

6 green onions, diced

1/3 head cabbage, sliced into long thin strips, or 2 to 3 c. shredded coleslaw mix

WASHINGTON WONDERS

With all the Asian influence in the state, one dish, pho soup, is a simple but tasty favorite. Ingredients can vary but it usually has chicken, rice, onion, cabbage and sometimes ginger or basil in the ingredients list.

CHILLED AVOCADO SOUP

JOYCE LAMURE
SEQUIM, WA

A neighbor gave me this refreshing recipe many years ago when we lived in Arizona. My family loved it on a hot summer night. Garnish with a dollop of sour cream and a sprinkle of chopped dill...delish!

1 cucumber, peeled, seeded and chopped

3 avocados, peeled, pitted and cubed

2 15-oz. cans chicken broth, divided

3/4 c. sour cream

3 T. lemon juice

1/8 t. hot pepper sauce

1-1/2 t. salt

1/2 to 2/3 c. half-and-half

1 Purée cucumber in a blender. Add avocado and purée again. Add one cup chicken broth and blend. Pour into a large bowl.

2 Add remaining broth and other ingredients except half-and-half. Stir well; thin to taste with half-and-half. Cover and chill; serve chilled.

Serves 4

KITCHEN TIP

To toast sesame seed place in a dry skillet over medium heat for 3 to 5 minutes, until lightly browned, stirring occasionally.

BEEF & MUSHROOM SOUP

WENDY TOP
SUNNYSIDE, WA

Add any of your favorite vegetables...potatoes, cabbage, beans, or corn. This soup is so easy to make that you will make it often!

1 In a large stockpot, sauté garlic, onion, carrot and celery in butter. Add beef, broth, bouillon, water and barley. Bring to a boil; boil for 3 minutes. Reduce heat to medium-low; stir in mushrooms. Simmer for 1-1/2 to 2 hours, adding more water if needed.

Makes 8 servings

2 cloves garlic, chopped
2 c. onion, chopped
1 c. carrot, peeled and sliced
1/2 c. celery, sliced
2 T. butter
1 lb. roast beef, coarsely chopped
3 c. beef broth
2 cubes beef bouillon
2 c. water
1/2 c. pearl barley, uncooked
1 lb. mushrooms, sliced

RASPBERRY VINAIGRETTE

MELODY TAYNOR
EVERETT, WA

Toss with bite-size fresh fruit for a refreshing summer salad.

1 Combine all ingredients in a blender; process until smooth. Cover; keep refrigerated.

Makes about 2-1/2 cups

1/4 c. olive oil
1 c. cider vinegar or seasoned rice vinegar
10-oz. jar seedless red raspberry jam

BUTTERNUT VEGGIE SOUP

SAMANTHA REILLY
GIG HARBOR, WA

An easy way to use butternut squash without a lot of squash flavor for those pickier eaters. Serve with biscuits or toast and butter.

1 butternut squash, peeled, seeded and cubed

2 c. cauliflower, cut into bite-size flowerets

1 T. olive oil

1 lb. ground beef

12 whole pearl onions, or 2 onions, chopped

28-oz. can crushed tomatoes

14-1/2 oz. can cut green beans, drained

11-oz. can corn, drained

4 c. water

3 T. beef soup base

3 T. fresh basil, chopped

2 T. fresh oregano, chopped

1 T. salt

1 t. pepper

1 Combine squash and cauliflower on a rimmed baking sheet; drizzle with oil. Bake, uncovered, at 350 degrees for about 30 minutes, until fork-tender; let cool.

2 Meanwhile, brown beef with onions in a large soup pot over medium heat; drain. Add squash mixture, tomatoes with juice and remaining ingredients to soup pot. Simmer until heated through, stirring occasionally, about 10 to 15 minutes.

Makes 8 to 10 servings

CHEESE & GARLIC CROUTONS

KENDALL HALE
LYNN, WA

These savory croutons are delicious sprinkled in a bowl of soup or tossed in a dinner salad.

1 Melt butter in a large skillet. Add seasonings, garlic and onion; cook for about one minute to soften. Stir in bread cubes; sauté until golden and crisp. Toss with cheese until coated. Cool; store in an airtight container.

Makes 2 cups

1/4 c. butter
1/2 t. dried oregano
1/2 t. dried basil
1/2 t. celery salt
2 cloves garlic, minced
1 T. onion, minced
2 c. whole-wheat bread, cubed
2 T. grated Parmesan cheese

PEPPER STEAK SAMMIES

VICKIE
GOOSEBERRY PATCH

Everyone loves a steak sandwich and this one won't disappoint. Enjoy!

1 Grill or broil steak to desired doneness; set aside. Sauté green peppers and onion in hot oil in a skillet over medium heat until crisp-tender; drain. Slice steak thinly; add to skillet and heat through. Sprinkle with salt and pepper.

2 Spread butter over cut sides of rolls. Spoon steak mixture onto bottom halves of rolls; cover with tops.

Makes 4 sandwiches

1 to 1-1/4 lbs. beef sirloin or ribeye steak
2 green peppers, thinly sliced
1 onion, sliced
1 T. oil
salt and pepper to taste
1/4 c. garlic butter, softened
4 French rolls, split and toasted

CHERRY TOMATO HUMMUS WRAPS

AMBER SUTTON
NACHES, WA

I love those little tomatoes that you can eat like candy straight from the vine! When I added garden-fresh basil and some other salad ingredients I had on hand, I was delightfully surprised with this resulting summer lunch.

4 T. hummus
4 8-inch flour tortillas, warmed
1 c. cherry tomatoes, halved
1/2 c. Kalamata olives, chopped
1/3 c. crumbled feta cheese
6 sprigs fresh basil, snipped

1 Spread one tablespoon hummus down the center of each tortilla. Divide remaining ingredients evenly over hummus.

2 To wrap up tortillas burrito-style, turn tortillas so that fillings are side-to-side. Fold in left and right sides of each tortilla; fold top and bottom edges over the filling.

Makes 4 servings

CHILLED APPLE & CHEESE SALAD

MELODY TAYNOR
EVERETT, WA

As a girl, I was convinced that I didn't like gelatin salads. But when my Aunt Clara served this at an anniversary party, I found I had been mistaken!

3-oz. pkg. lemon gelatin mix
1 c. boiling water
3/4 c. cold water
2/3 c. red apple, cored and finely chopped
1/3 c. shredded Cheddar cheese
1/4 c. celery, chopped

1 In a bowl, dissolve gelatin in boiling water. Stir in cold water; chill until partially set. Fold in remaining ingredients. Pour into a 3-cup mold. Cover and chill 3 hours, or until firm. Unmold onto a serving plate

Makes 6 servings

MEXICAN CONFETTI SALAD

VICKIE
GOOSEBERRY PATCH

*We all love this fresh-tasting salad! I like to use
red or yellow peppers for color when they're on sale.
Or sometimes I find the perfect ones at the farmers' market.*

1 Combine all ingredients in a serving bowl. Drizzle
with Lime Dressing; toss gently. Chill until serving
time.

Serves 6

3 c. frozen corn, cooked
and drained
3 tomatoes, chopped
2 green peppers, chopped
15-oz. can black beans,
drained and rinsed
1/3 c. fresh cilantro,
chopped

1 Combine all ingredients in a tight-lidded jar; cover
and shake to mix.

LIME DRESSING:
3 T. lime juice
1 t. garlic, minced
1 t. salt
1 t. pepper
1/4 c. olive oil

VEGGIE PATCH STEW

WENDY TOP
SUNNYSIDE, WA

*This yummy stew uses just about every vegetable from our garden.
That is how it got its name! If we don't have the veggies we want,
we make a trip to the farmers' market. They have everything here!*

3 zucchini, sliced
3 yellow squash, sliced
2 onions, chopped
2 tomatoes, chopped
1 eggplant, peeled and
  cubed
1 green pepper, chopped
1 clove garlic, minced
1 T. butter, softened
1 t. hot pepper sauce
1/2 t. curry powder
1 t. chili powder
salt and pepper to taste
Garnish: shredded
  mozzarella cheese

1 Place all vegetables in a large Dutch oven over low heat. Stir in remaining ingredients except cheese.

2 Cover and simmer for one hour, stirring frequently. Do not add any liquid, as vegetables make their own juices. Top portions with cheese before serving if desired.

Makes 6 servings

KITCHEN TIP

When refrigerating leftover dressings, keep in jars or bottles marked with the name of the dressing and the date that it was refrigerated.

34 ALL-TIME-FAVORITE RECIPES FROM *Washington* WASHINGTON COOKS

CHINESE COLESLAW

CAROLYN AYERS
KENT, WA

This salad is crunchy, colorful and full of flavor, but it's the dressing that really makes this a stand-out! Toasting the sesame seed brings out the nutty flavor. Yummy!

1 Combine the cabbage, pepper, pea pods, bean sprouts and onions in a large bowl. Drizzle with Sesame-Ginger Dressing; toss and sprinkle with sesame seed. Toss once more before serving.

Makes 12 servings

9 c. Napa cabbage, shredded

4 c. green cabbage, shredded

1 c. red or green pepper, sliced

1 c. snow pea pods

1 c. bean sprouts

5 green onions, sliced

Garnish: 2 T. toasted sesame seed

1 Combine all ingredients in a jar with a tight-fitting lid. Secure lid and shake well to blend.

SESAME-GINGER DRESSING:

1 clove garlic, minced

1/8-inch thick slice fresh ginger, peeled and minced

1/4 c. sesame seed oil or peanut oil

3 T. soy sauce

3 T. rice wine vinegar

1 t. sugar

Optional: 4 drops chili oil

COLBY CORN CHOWDER

VICKIE
GOOSEBERRY PATCH

This recipe makes a large batch of soup that works great for big family gatherings or soup suppers for holiday events. It is quick to make and everyone always loves it!

6 potatoes, peeled and
  cubed
1 t. salt
1 onion, chopped
1/4 c. butter
2 14-3/4 oz. cans
  creamed corn
4 slices bacon, cooked
  and crisply crumbled
3 c. milk
8-oz. pkg. Colby cheese,
  cubed

1 Place potatoes in a soup pot; sprinkle with salt and cover with water. Bring to a boil over medium heat. Cover and simmer until potatoes are tender.

2 Meanwhile, in a skillet over medium heat, sauté onion in butter until tender. Stir in corn and bacon; heat through. Drain potatoes; return to pot. Add milk and heat through over low heat. Stir in corn mixture and cheese; stir until cheese is melted. Serve immediately.

Makes 12 to 14 servings

NO-PEEK STEW

MARY JO URBANIAK
SPOKANE, WA

The hard part is not peeking!

1 T. olive oil
2-1/2 lbs. stew beef cubes
2 onions, quartered
4 stalks celery, chopped
4 potatoes, peeled and
  cubed
3 carrots, peeled and
  sliced
2 t. pearl tapioca,
  uncooked
1 T. sugar
salt and pepper to taste
10-3/4 oz. can tomato
  soup
1-1/4 c. water
10-oz. pkg. frozen peas

1 Add oil to Dutch oven. Add beef cubes and cook until lightly browned.

2 Add the remaining ingredients in order listed to the Dutch oven; cover. Bake at 325 degrees for 4 hours.

Serves 4

GRILLED GRECIAN SALAD PIZZA

**LISA KASTNING
MARYSVILLE, WA**

Such a fun pizza! I make it for my sister-in-law who's a vegetarian, but no one misses the meat anyway. Serve it as a main dish or cut into smaller portions to serve as an appetizer.

1 Heat 1-1/2 tablespoons olive oil in a large skillet over medium heat. Add garlic; sauté until lightly golden. Add lettuce and lemon juice to skillet; stir quickly, just until lettuce is wilted. Brush remaining olive oil over pizza crusts. Top with tomatoes, lettuce mixture and remaining ingredients.

2 Place pizzas on a grill over medium-high heat; close cover. Cook until crusts are golden, vegetables are heated through and cheese is beginning to melt. Cut into wedges.

Makes 12 to 16 servings

3 T. olive oil, divided

4 cloves garlic, minced

3 c. romaine lettuce, shredded

1 T. lemon juice

2 12-inch pre-baked Italian pizza crusts

2 to 3 tomatoes, thinly sliced

1-1/2 c. crumbled feta cheese

6 to 8 pepperoncini, chopped

1 c. chopped black olives

2 T. fresh oregano, minced

cracked pepper to taste

WASHINGTON WONDERS

Ivar's Seafood Restaurant and Clam Chowder, started in 1938, is famous for its fish and chips and, of course, chowder.

HAEGEN'S BEEF STEW

KRYS LEWIS
VANCOUVER, WA

*This hearty, filling recipe was handed down from my grandma.
The first time my children tried it, my oldest son liked it so much
that he named it after himself!*

1 lb. ground beef
5 potatoes, peeled and
  cubed
4 c. water
15-oz. can peas, drained
  and liquid reserved
1 cube beef bouillon
1 T. onion powder
1/8 t. salt
1/2 c. all-purpose flour

1 Brown beef in a stockpot over medium heat; drain.
Add potatoes, water, reserved liquid from peas,
bouillon, onion powder and salt.

2 Simmer until potatoes are soft, about 30 minutes.
Stir in flour; if needed, add a little more water to
make a light gravy. After gravy has simmered for a
few minutes, gently stir in peas. Let simmer for a few
minutes before serving.

Serves 4 to 6

SUNNY QUINOA SALAD

JO ANN
GOOSEBERRY PATCH

*With its bright flavors, this good-for-you salad makes a yummy
lunch!*

2 c. quinoa, uncooked
2-1/2 c. chicken broth
4 green onions, thinly
  sliced
1/2 c. golden raisins,
  chopped
2 T. rice vinegar
1/2 c. orange juice
1 t. orange zest
2 T. olive oil
1/4 t. ground cumin
1 cucumber, peeled and
  chopped
1/2 c. fresh flat-leaf
  parsley, chopped
salt and pepper to taste

1 Rinse quinoa under cold water until water runs
clear. In a saucepan, bring chicken broth to a boil.
Add quinoa; return to a boil.

2 Cover and simmer until quinoa has fully expanded,
about 20 to 25 minutes. Remove from heat; fluff
with a fork. In a large bowl, combine quinoa and
remaining ingredients; mix well. Cover and chill
before serving.

Serves 6 to 8

HAM & POTATO SOUP

TIFFANY BURDETTE
EVERSON, WA

After a big family Easter dinner, there was so much ham left, I didn't know what to do with it! This satisfying soup recipe was just right. Save room for seconds, because you'll definitely want more! This soup freezes and reheats really well.

1 In a slow cooker, combine all ingredients except butter, flour and milk. Cover and cook on low setting for 6 to 8 hours, until potatoes are fork-tender.

2 About 20 minutes before serving, melt butter in a saucepan over medium heat; stir in flour. Gradually add milk, stirring constantly until thickened. Stir mixture into soup in slow cooker. Cover and cook on low setting an additional 15 to 20 minutes, until thickened.

Makes 8 servings

3-1/2 c. potatoes, peeled and diced
1/3 c. celery, chopped
1/3 c. onion, finely chopped
3/4 c. cooked ham, diced
3-1/4 c. water
6 cubes chicken bouillon
1/2 t. salt
1 t. pepper
5 T. butter
5 T. all-purpose flour
2 c. milk

PRESENTATION

Serve soup in hearty bread bowls. Simply hollow out the center of round loaves of your favorite crusty bread, leaving the bottom crust.

HEARTY BEEF STEW

KATHLEEN KENNEDY
RENTON, WA

*I like to serve this slow-cooker stew with warm biscuits
for an easy meal that kids and guys love.*

2 lbs. stew beef cubes
1/2 c. all-purpose flour
salt and pepper to taste
4 T. oil, divided
4 potatoes, peeled and
cubed
6 carrots, peeled and
cubed
1-3/4 c. canned diced
tomatoes
2 0.87-oz. envs. brown
gravy mix
10-3/4 oz. can cream of
mushroom soup
2 c. beef broth or water

1 Pat beef dry with paper towels; set aside.
Combine flour, salt and pepper in a plastic zipping
bag. In small batches, toss beef in bag to coat.

2 In a heavy skillet, heat 2 tablespoons oil over
medium-high heat. Add beef to skillet in batches,
browning on all sides; add a little more oil as
needed. Drain; season beef with additional salt and
pepper.

3 Transfer beef to a slow cooker; add vegetables. In
a bowl, whisk together remaining ingredients. Pour
gravy mixture over all; gently stir to mix. Cover and
cook on low setting for 8 to 10 hours.

Serves 6

CHEESY ZUCCHINI JOES

NOLA COONS
GOOSEBERRY PATCH

*This vegetarian sandwich is sure to become a favorite for the
entire family. They won't miss the meat!*

2 T. butter
2 zucchini, halved and
sliced
1/8 t. red pepper flakes
1/8 t. garlic powder
salt and pepper to taste
1 c. marinara or
spaghetti sauce
1 c. shredded mozzarella
cheese
4 6-inch wheat sub
rolls, split

1 Melt butter in a skillet over medium heat. Fry
zucchini in butter until golden and slightly tender.
Add seasonings. Stir in sauce. Cook and stir until
sauce is heated through.

2 For each sandwich, spoon a generous amount of
zucchini mixture onto bottom half of bun. Sprinkle
with cheese and replace bun top. Wrap sandwiches
individually in aluminum foil. Place on a baking sheet
and bake at 350 degrees for 15 minutes, or until
heated through and cheese is melted.

Makes 4 servings

MINTY MELON SALAD

VICKIE
GOOSEBERRY PATCH

The spicy, fresh mint really brings out the sweetness of the juicy melon in this bright & cheery salad.

1 Combine water, sugar, juice and mint in a saucepan; bring to a boil. Boil for 2 minutes, stirring constantly. Remove from heat; cover and cool completely. Combine fruit in a large bowl. Pour cooled dressing over fruit; stir until well coated. Cover and chill for at least 2 hours, stirring occasionally. Drain liquid before serving. Garnish with fresh mint sprigs.

Serves 10

1 c. water
3/4 c. sugar
3 T. lime juice
1-1/2 t. fresh mint, chopped
5 c. watermelon, cubed
3 c. cantaloupe, cubed
3 c. honeydew, cubed
2 c. nectarines, pitted and sliced
1 c. blueberries
Garnish: fresh mint sprigs

HERBED CHERRY TOMATOES

DEBBIE PRIVETT
TACOMA, WA

This is a recipe my mom got from her own mother. My family can't wait to make it each summer! We enjoy these tomatoes served over a scoop of cottage cheese.

1 Place tomatoes in a serving bowl; set aside. In a separate bowl, whisk together remaining ingredients. Drizzle oil mixture over tomatoes and mix well. For the best flavor, cover and refrigerate up to 24 hours before serving.

Serves 4

2 c. cherry tomatoes, sliced
1/4 c. oil
3 T. red wine vinegar
1/4 c. fresh parsley, snipped
1/2 t. dried basil
1/2 t. dried oregano
1/2 t. salt
1/2 t. sugar

ICEBOX CARROT SALAD

SUSAN HATFIELD
PASCO, WA

This is one of my favorite salads. My mother-in-law shared this recipe with me years ago.

1/2 c. oil
3/4 c. vinegar
11-oz. can tomato bisque soup
1 c. sugar
1 t. Worcestershire sauce
1 t. pepper
1 t. dry mustard
5 c. carrots, peeled, sliced and cooked
1 onion, sliced
1 green pepper, chopped

1 Combine oil, vinegar, soup, sugar, Worcestershire sauce and spices in a saucepan over medium-high heat. Bring to a boil. Remove from heat and pour over vegetables. Cover and refrigerate overnight.

Makes 6 to 8 servings

MICKY'S CRUNCHY SWEET-AND-SOUR SLAW

ROSALIND DICKINSON
GRANDVIEW, WA

A family friend came up with this quick & easy summer salad one night when he and my hubby were barbecuing together. Since then, it's become a favorite. My sorority sisters have even requested my husband to make it for our get-togethers.

16-oz. pkg. shredded coleslaw mix
16-oz. pkg. shredded broccoli-carrot coleslaw mix
3/4 c. mayonnaise
1/2 c. cider vinegar
1/4 t. garlic salt
1/2 t. pepper
1 c. tomato, diced

1 Toss together coleslaw mixes in a serving bowl; set aside. In a small bowl, stir together remaining ingredients except tomato. Add to coleslaw mixture and toss to coat well. Gently fold in tomato. Serve immediately, or cover and refrigerate until serving time.

Makes 12 servings

ONE-HOUR WILD RICE SOUP

LINDSEY ELLINGSEN
MILTON, WA

My mom used to make this soup for us during cold weather. Once I made it for my husband when I was feeling a little homesick, and he said, "Why on earth have we never had this before?!" Now he asks for this soup all through autumn and winter. It tastes wonderful served in sourdough bread bowls.

1 Cook wild rice in broth, according to package directions. This may take from 45 to 55 minutes at a simmer. Do not drain.

2 Meanwhile, warm olive oil in a soup pot over medium-high heat. Add celery, carrots, onion and peppers; sauté until crisp-tender. Add seasonings, cooked rice and soup to vegetables. Cook, stirring often, until bubbly and heated through.

Serves 4 to 6

1 c. wild rice, uncooked

32-oz. container chicken or vegetable broth

1 T. olive oil

3 stalks celery, chopped

3 carrots, peeled and chopped

1/2 c. onion, chopped

1 green pepper, chopped

2 t. jalapeño pepper, minced

1 t. dried rosemary

1 t. dried thyme

pepper to taste

2 23-oz. cans cream of mushroom soup

VEGGIE MELTS

JO ANN
GOOSEBERRY PATCH

For a little spice, add a little fresh basil to this already-delightful sandwich.

1 c. sliced baby
  portabella mushrooms
1/4 c. olive oil
1 loaf ciabatta bread,
  halved horizontally
8-oz. jar whole roasted
  red peppers, drained
1-1/2 t. Italian seasoning
1 c. shredded Fontina
  cheese

1 In a skillet over medium heat, sauté mushrooms in olive oil until tender. Place bread halves on an ungreased baking sheet. On one bread half, layer peppers, mushrooms and Italian seasoning. Top both halves evenly with cheese.

2 Broil until lightly golden. Assemble sandwich and cut into 4 pieces.

Makes 4 servings

PRESENTATION

Choose wood cutting boards to use as serving trays to present your sandwiches. Place a sheet of natural parchment paper under each sandwich.

MOM'S CHAMPION CHICKEN SOUP

MELODY TAYNOR
EVERETT, WA

Guaranteed to chase away the chills! For extra goodness, use homemade chicken broth...you'll need about 10 cups.

1 Melt butter in a stockpot over medium heat. Sauté onion and celery in butter until just tender, about 5 minutes. Pour in broth; add remaining ingredients except noodles.

2 Bring to a boil; stir in noodles. Reduce heat slightly and simmer for 15 to 20 minutes, until noodles are tender.

Makes 6 servings

1 T. butter
1/2 c. onion, chopped
1/2 c. celery, chopped
2 32-oz. containers chicken broth
14-1/2 oz. can chicken broth
1 c. cooked chicken, diced
1 c. carrots, peeled and sliced
2 t. dried parsley
salt and pepper to taste
1-1/2 c. thin egg noodles, uncooked

CHAPTER THREE

DELIGHTFUL
Dinnertime

PULL UP A CHAIR AND GATHER
WITH FAMILY & FRIENDS TO
ENJOY A TASTY HOME-COOKED
DINNER USING MARKET-FRESH
INGREDIENTS THAT ARE SURE
TO PLEASE.

MUSHROOM-MOZZARELLA BAKE

**DANA ROWAN
SPOKANE, WA**

*Sautéed mushrooms in butter, cream and herbs, topped with
mozzarella cheese and baked until melty...what's not to love about that?
Serve by itself or spooned over a grilled steak. So delicious!*

1 lb. sliced mushrooms
3 T. butter
1/2 t. seasoning salt
2 T. whipping cream
1 t. dried parsley
1/4 t. pepper
3/4 to 1 c. shredded
   mozzarella cheese

1 In a skillet over medium heat, sauté mushrooms in butter until softened. Keep cooking until most of the liquid evaporates. Add seasoning salt; continue to sauté until mushrooms are golden. Reduce heat to low; stir in cream, parsley and pepper. Simmer until cream is slightly reduced.

2 Transfer mushroom mixture to an ungreased shallow 2-quart casserole dish. Sprinkle with cheese. Bake, uncovered, at 350 degrees for 10 minutes, or until cheese is melted.

Serves 4 to 6

PORK CHOP BUNDLES

**KAREN OVERHOLT
KENNEWICK, WA**

*When my kids were home, we always had fun fixing dinner
together and coming up with different ideas. This tasty recipe is
my son Cory's creation.*

1 bone-in pork chop,
   1/2-inch thick
salt and pepper to taste
1/2 t. oil
1 potato, thinly sliced
1/2 onion, thinly sliced
1 fresh or frozen ear
   corn on the cob, husks
   and silk removed
Optional: 2 to 3 ice cubes

1 Season pork chop with salt and pepper. Heat oil in a skillet over medium-high heat; brown chop on both sides. Layer chop and remaining ingredients on a 14-inch length of heavy-duty aluminum foil in order listed, seasoning with more salt and pepper. Add ice cubes, if fresh corn is used. Wrap securely.

2 Cover and grill over medium-high heat for about one hour. May also bake on a baking sheet at 350 degrees for one hour.

Serves one

SOUR CREAM SPAGHETTI

PATRICIA MARZWICK
OLYMPIA, WA

My mother-in-law shared this recipe with me. It makes quite a lot, so it's great for a potluck or a gathering of friends. I serve a crisp salad and garlic bread to complete the meal.

1 Cook noodles according to package directions; drain. Meanwhile, brown beef in a large skillet over medium heat; drain. Add onion, garlic, sugar and seasonings to beef; stir in tomato sauce.

2 Simmer over low heat for 15 minutes, stirring occasionally. Add cream cheese and sour cream; mix well. Gently fold in cooked noodles

3 Layer half of noodle mixture and half of shredded cheese in a greased deep 13"x9" baking pan. Repeat layers. Bake, uncovered, at 350 degrees for 35 to 45 minutes, until bubbly and cheese is melted.

Makes 8 to 10 servings

10-oz. pkg. medium egg noodles, uncooked

2 lbs. ground beef

1 onion, chopped

2 cloves garlic, minced

1 t. sugar

1 t. salt

pepper to taste

2 15-oz. cans tomato sauce

8-oz. pkg. cream cheese, softened

16-oz. container sour cream

2 c. shredded Cheddar cheese, divided

SPICY BEEF CASSEROLE

KAREN WILLIAMS
PORT ORCHARD, WA

Ideal for toting to an office potluck or luncheon.

1 lb. ground beef
1 onion, chopped
salt and pepper to taste
4-oz. can diced green
  chiles
3 c. shredded Cheddar
  cheese, divided
1/4 c. all-purpose flour
1/2 t. salt
4 eggs
1-1/2 c. milk
1/2 t. hot pepper sauce

1 Brown beef with onion; drain. Sprinkle with salt and pepper; set aside. Layer chiles in an ungreased 13"x9" baking pan; top with half the beef mixture and half the cheese. Repeat layers; set aside.

2 Whisk together remaining ingredients; pour on top. Bake at 350 degrees until set, about 45 minutes.

Serves 6

ROASTED NEW POTATOES

MELANIE TAYNOR
EVERETT, WA

Better than hashbrowns! Garnish with sprigs of fresh rosemary.

1/4 c. butter, melted
garlic powder, seasoned
  salt and pepper to
  taste
2 t. fresh rosemary
1-1/2 lbs. new potatoes,
  cut into wedges

1 In a shallow 13"x9" baking pan, combine butter and seasonings. Add potatoes; stir to coat evenly. Arrange the potatoes in a single layer.

2 Bake, uncovered, at 350 degrees until potatoes are golden, about 20 to 25 minutes, stirring occasionally.

Makes 4 servings.

SPINACH & PROVOLONE-STUFFED CHICKEN

KENDALL HALE
LYNN, WA

This dish looks as if it took all day to make, but it really doesn't take long at all. Serve with some fresh asparagus and a salad for a beautiful meal.

1 Pound chicken flat; sprinkle with pepper. Place one slice of prosciutto on top of each chicken breast. Spread spinach evenly over prosciutto; sprinkle with Parmesan cheese. Top each chicken breast with a slice of provolone cheese and roll up, starting at tapered end. Secure each roll with a toothpick.

2 Heat oil in a skillet over medium-high heat. Cook rolls in oil, turning once, until golden on both sides, about 8 minutes. Add broth and bring to a boil. Reduce heat to medium-low; cover and simmer for 10 minutes, or until chicken is no longer pink in the center.

3 Transfer rolls to a serving plate; keep warm. Increase heat to high; cook until liquid in skillet is thickened. Drizzle sauce over rolls.

Serves 4

1 lb. boneless, skinless chicken breasts

1/4 t. pepper

4 thin slices prosciutto ham

10-oz. pkg. frozen chopped spinach, thawed and drained

1/4 c. grated Parmesan cheese

2 slices provolone cheese, halved

1 T. olive oil

14-1/2 oz. can chicken broth

ASIAN COUNTRY-STYLE RIBS

MELODY TAYNOR
EVERETT, WA

*For a super-easy side, steam a package of frozen stir-fry veggies...
top with crunchy chow mein noodles. Dinner is served!*

4 lbs. boneless country-
  style pork ribs
1/4 c. brown sugar,
  packed
1 c. soy sauce
1/4 c. sesame oil
2 T. olive oil
2 T. rice vinegar
2 T. lime juice
2 T. garlic, minced
2 T. fresh ginger, peeled
  and grated
1 t. hot pepper sauce
cooked rice

1 Place ribs in a large plastic zipping bag. Stir together remaining ingredients except rice; pour over ribs. Seal bag and refrigerate for 8 hours to overnight, turning bag occasionally to coat ribs with marinade. Drain marinade and discard; place ribs in a slow cooker.

2 Cover and cook on low setting for 8 to 9 hours, until tender. Drain; shred ribs using 2 forks. Serve over cooked rice.

Serves 6

AUTUMN APPLE-PECAN DRESSING

FAWN MCKENZIE
WENATCHEE, WA

Made in the slow cooker, this side dish frees up your oven for a tasty roast chicken.

1 Combine bread cubes, cracker crumbs, apples, pecans, onion and celery in a slow cooker; set aside. In a small bowl, mix remaining ingredients until well blended.

2 Pour into slow cooker and toss to coat. Cover and cook on low setting for 4 to 5 hours, until dressing is puffed and golden around the edges.

Serves 8

4 c. soft bread cubes

1 c. saltine crackers, crushed

1-1/2 c. apples, peeled, cored and chopped

1 c. chopped pecans

1 c. onion, chopped

1 c. celery, chopped

2/3 c. chicken broth

1/4 c. butter, melted

2 eggs, beaten

1/2 t. pepper

1/2 t. dried sage

WASHINGTON WONDERS

Washington residents celebrate their growing seasons. There's a Northwest Raspberry Festival at Lynden, a National Lentil Festival in Pullman, Wenatchee River Salmon Festival and Issaquah Salmon Days Festival. Plus, there's the Sweet Onion Festival in Walla Walla.

AUTUMN APPLE PORK ROAST

VICKIE
GOOSEBERRY PATCH

*Add a side of sauerkraut and some creamy mashed potatoes...
a perfect meal for those cool fall days!*

4-lb. pork loin roast
salt and pepper to taste
6 tart apples, cored and
  quartered
1/4 c. apple juice
3 T. brown sugar,
  packed
1 t. ground ginger

1 Rub roast with salt and pepper. Brown roast under a broiler to remove excess fat; drain. Place apples in the bottom of a slow cooker. Place roast on top of apples. Mix together remaining ingredients and spoon over roast. Cover and cook on low setting for 8 to 10 hours.

Makes 6 to 8 servings

ROZ'S BRUNCH CASSEROLE

ROSALIND DICKINSON
GRANDVIEW, WA

My husband's family has a Thanksgiving brunch every year, and I'm required to bring this delicious dish...it's a real favorite! I love that I can dice the veggies and ham the night before, then in the morning it takes only ten minutes to pop it in the oven. Even the warmed-up leftovers taste fantastic!

1/2 c. onion, diced
1/2 c. green pepper, diced
1 to 2 t. oil
2 c. cooked ham, diced
1 doz. eggs, beaten
1 c. milk
32-oz. pkg. frozen
  shredded potatoes
1 c. shredded Cheddar
  cheese
seasoning salt or salt-
  free seasoning blend to
  taste
pepper to taste
Garnish: additional
  shredded Cheddar
  cheese

1 In a skillet over medium heat, cook onion and green pepper in oil until softened. Add ham and warm through; remove from heat. In a large bowl, stir together eggs, milk, frozen potatoes, onion mixture and cheese. Add seasonings to taste.

2 Pour into a lightly greased 13"x9" baking pan, spreading evenly. Bake, uncovered, at 350 degrees for 45 minutes to one hour, until set. Top with additional cheese.

Serves 10 to 15

BEN GETTY CASSEROLE

WHITLEY SAKAS
SEQUIM, WA

During the Second World War, my parents were in the Air Force and food was limited. Colonel Ben Getty was one of my parents' best friends and he would bring over his family to share a double batch of this delicious casserole with our own family. It didn't have a name, so we named it after him. I hope you'll enjoy this dish as much as we have!

1 In a large skillet over medium heat, brown beef or turkey with onion and green pepper, if using. Drain; add salt and pepper. Stir in cooked macaroni and soups; gently fold in undrained peas.

2 Pour all into a lightly greased 13"x9" baking pan and cover. Bake at 350 degrees for 50 to 60 minutes, until bubbly. Uncover; arrange cheese slices on top and return to oven until melted, about 5 minutes.

Serves 4 to 6

1 lb. lean ground beef or turkey

1/4 c. onion, chopped

Optional: 1/4 c. green pepper, chopped

salt and pepper to taste

7-oz. pkg. elbow macaroni, cooked

10-3/4 oz. can cream of mushroom soup

10-3/4 oz. can tomato soup

8-1/2 oz. can petite peas

6 slices pasteurized process cheese

CARLY'S POT O' BEANS

CARLY ST. CLAIR
LYNNWOOD, WA

This is comfort food at our home. On a cold autumn or winter evening after a long day at work, it's heavenly to come home to the aroma of these beans simmering in the slow cooker. Serve with homemade cornbread or biscuits.

2 16-oz. pkg's. dried
  pinto beans
1-1/2 c. celery with
  leaves, chopped
3 carrots, peeled and
  chopped, or 1 c. baby
  carrots, chopped
1 onion, chopped
8 c. chicken broth
1 env. ham seasoning
  concentrate
1 t. garlic powder
1/4 t. pepper

1 In a large bowl, cover dried beans with water. Let soak overnight. In the morning, drain and rinse beans. Add beans to a slow cooker sprayed with non-stick vegetable spray. Add celery, carrots and onion; pour broth over all. Add remaining ingredients; stir until blended.

2 Cover and cook on high setting for 6 to 8 hours, until beans are soft.

Makes 12 servings

WASHINGTON WONDERS

While many state fairs around the country have long lines at the funnel cake or corn dog stands, the Washington State Fair in Puyallup has long lines for scones. They are served warm and filled with butter and raspberry jam.

CAULIFLOWER FRIED RICE

ANNETTE MCDONALD
TACOMA, WA

This is a fun recipe! Always counting carbs, our family loves this dish and we tweak it to fit our various tastes. Feel free to add bamboo shoots, water chestnuts, sliced celery, broccoli flowerets or other veggies. This can easily become a main dish by adding chopped cooked meat, shrimp or tofu.

1 In a large skillet, heat sesame oil and 3 teaspoons canola oil over medium-high heat. Add onion; sauté for 2 to 4 minutes. Add peas and mushrooms; cook an additional 3 to 5 minutes, stirring often.

2 Meanwhile, in a separate small skillet over low heat, lightly scramble egg in remaining canola oil. Add cauliflower, soy sauce and scrambled egg to mixture in large skillet. Cook 5 to 8 minutes more, stirring often. Serve garnished with chopped green onions.

Makes 4 servings

- 1/2 t. sesame oil
- 4 t. canola oil, divided
- 1/2 c. onion, chopped
- 1/2 c. fresh or frozen peas or snow peas
- 1/2 c. mushrooms, thinly sliced
- 1 egg, beaten
- 3-1/2 c. fresh cauliflower, grated
- 2 T. light soy sauce
- Garnish: 2 green onions, chopped

CHEESY CHICKEN & TOTS CASSEROLE

DANA ROWAN
SPOKANE, WA

This recipe can be put together in a jiffy, as I always have the ingredients on hand. Feel free to use your own favorite cheese.

32-oz. pkg. frozen potato
  puffs, divided
1 to 1-1/2 3-oz. pkgs.
  ready-to-use bacon
  pieces, divided
2 c. shredded sharp
  Cheddar cheese
1 lb. boneless, skinless
  chicken breast, diced
garlic salt and
  Montreal steak
  seasoning or salt and
  pepper to taste
3/4 c. milk

1 To a slow cooker sprayed with non-stick vegetable spray, add half of the frozen potato puffs. Sprinkle with 1/3 each of bacon pieces and cheese. Add chicken; season as desired. Top with another 1/3 each of bacon and cheese.

2 Arrange remaining potato puffs, bacon and cheese on top. Pour milk evenly over the top. Cover and cook on low setting for 4 to 6 hours.

Makes 6 to 8 servings

CHEESY POTATO BAKE

HOLLY COREY
BURIEN, WA

I love serving this for brunch…a hit with family & friends!

1 Combine first 6 ingredients; spread in a buttered 13"x9" baking pan. Set aside. Toss remaining ingredients together; sprinkle over potato mixture. Bake at 350 degrees for 30 to 40 minutes.

Serves 8

32-oz. pkg. frozen diced potatoes, thawed
1 c. shredded Colby Jack Cheese
10-3/4 oz. can cream of mushroom soup
10-3/4 oz. can cream of potato soup
1/2 c. sour cream
1/2 c. mayonnaise
1-1/2 c. corn flake cereal
1/4 to 1/2 c. butter, melted
1/2 c. grated Parmesan cheese

SALMON-STUFFED TOMATOES

SYLVIA MATHEWS
VANCOUVER, WA

Traditional stuffed tomatoes "dressed-up" with salmon and capers.

1 Scoop out and discard tomato pulp; set aside. Combine remaining ingredients; evenly spoon into tomato halves.

2 Place on a lightly greased baking sheet. Bake at 350 degrees for 30 minutes.

Serves 2

1 tomato, halved
1/2 lb. salmon, chopped
1/3 c. bread crumbs
1/2 c. fresh Italian parsley, chopped
1 t. olive oil
1 clove garlic, chopped
1 to 2 t. capers, chopped

CHICKEN & CORNBREAD BAKE

**TRACY BRUCE
MCCHORD AFB, WA**

Tender chicken between layers of buttery cornbread.

**2 to 3 7-oz. pkgs.
cornbread mix**

1 onion diced

2 T. butter

**2 boneless, skinless
chicken breasts, cooked
and cubed**

**10-3/4 oz. can cream of
chicken soup**

**10-3/4 oz. can cream of
celery soup**

**10-1/2 oz. can chicken
broth**

**3 eggs, hard-boiled,
peeled and sliced**

1 Prepare and bake cornbread according to package directions; crumble and set aside. Sauté onion in butter until tender; add cornbread, mixing well. Remove from heat; spread half the cornbread mixture in an ungreased 13"x9" baking pan. Set aside.

2 Combine chicken, soups and broth; pour over cornbread mixture. Arrange egg slices on top; spread remaining cornbread mixture over the top. Bake at 325 degrees until heated through, about 20 to 30 minutes.

Serves 8 to 10

CHICKEN & PARSLEY DUMPLINGS

KATHLEEN KENNEDY
RENTON, WA

This is my go-to dish when the family is gathered together in the fall and winter. I've been making this dinner over 30 years, so you know it's tried & true!

1 In a stockpot, cover chicken pieces with water; add vegetables and salt. Bring to a boil over high heat; reduce heat to low. Cover and simmer for 2-1/2 to 3 hours, until chicken is very tender; do not boil.

2 Remove chicken and vegetables to a large bowl, reserving broth. Discard bones and skin from chicken; keep chicken and vegetables warm. Strain broth and measure; add enough water to equal 3 cups.

3 Return broth to pan along with chicken and vegetables; bring to a boil. Combine milk and flour in a covered jar; shake until smooth. Add slowly to broth, stirring with a whisk. Drop dough for Parsley Dumplings into broth by tablespoonfuls. Simmer, uncovered, for 10 minutes. Cover; simmer another 10 minutes.

Serves 4 to 6

4 to 5-lb. stewing chicken, cut up
2 carrots, peeled and sliced
1 onion, sliced
1 stalk celery, sliced
1 t. salt
1 c. milk
1/3 c. all-purpose flour

1 Stir together flour, baking powder and salt; add parsley. Cut in shortening with a fork until mixture resembles cornmeal. Stir in milk until a soft dough forms.

PARSLEY DUMPLINGS:

2 c. all-purpose flour
1 T. baking powder
1 t. salt
1/4 c. fresh parsley, chopped
1/4 c. shortening
1 c. milk

CHICKEN TURNOVERS

ANGELA BETTENCOURT
MUKILTEO, WA

This is one of the most requested recipes in our family of five hungry boys...a 13-year-old and four (yes, quadruplets!) 10-year-olds. It is definitely comfort food and we hope everyone who tries it will enjoy it! I double this recipe to feed my hungry crew.

4 c. cooked chicken, cubed

8-oz. pkg. cream cheese, softened

1/2 c. milk

1 T. onion, minced

1 t. salt

1/8 t. pepper

2 8-oz. tubes refrigerated crescent rolls

1 T. butter, melted

3/4 c. grated Parmesan cheese

2 10-3/4 oz. cans cream of chicken soup

2/3 c. milk

1 Blend chicken, cream cheese, milk, onion, salt and pepper; set aside. Separate each tube of crescent rolls into 4 rectangles; press to seal perforations.

2 Spoon 1/2 cup chicken mixture into center of each rectangle; pull up corners to form a triangle and press to seal.

3 Place turnovers on an ungreased baking sheet. Brush tops with butter; sprinkle with Parmesan. Bake, uncovered, at 350 degrees for 20 to 25 minutes, until golden. While turnovers are baking, combine soup and milk in a saucepan; heat until bubbly. Spoon soup mixture over turnovers.

Serves 4 to 6

CHICKEN-BACON SANDWICH SPREAD

ROSALIND DICKINSON
GRANDVIEW, WA

This makes a delicious and healthy sandwich...kids love it! Spread it on crackers for an appetizer or spoon it onto crisp romaine lettuce for a salad. Sometimes I'll change up the cheese...Pepper Jack is great for adding a little zip and blue cheese crumbles are tasty too

1 In a bowl, combine chicken, bacon, onion and 1/3 cup salad dressing. Stir; add remaining dressing to desired consistency. More dressing may be added to make a spread for crackers. Season to taste with herb seasoning.

2 To serve, spread chicken mixture on bread; add cheese and lettuce, if desired.

Serves 4 to 5

2 boneless, skinless chicken breasts, cooked and diced or shredded

1/3 c. bacon, crisply cooked and crumbled, or bacon bits

1/4 c. sweet onion, finely chopped

2/3 c. mayonnaise-type salad dressing

herb seasoning to taste

8 to 10 slices multigrain bread

Optional: 4 to 6 cheese slices, romaine lettuce

CITRUS-GRILLED
PORK TENDERLOIN

JO ANN
GOOSEBERRY PATCH

These little medallions of tenderloin are so tasty with the sweet orange marmalade marinade. We like them with grilled potatoes.

1 lb. pork tenderloin,
  sliced 3/4-inch thick
1/2 t. pepper
2/3 c. orange
  marmalade
1/4 c. fresh mint,
  chopped
1/4 c. soy sauce
4 cloves garlic, minced

1 Sprinkle pork slices with pepper. Combine remaining ingredients; stir well. Brush over pork, reserving remaining marmalade mixture. Place pork on a lightly greased grill over high heat; grill for 3 minutes per side, or until no longer pink. Baste frequently with reserved marmalade mixture. Place marmalade mixture in a saucepan and bring to a boil over medium heat; cook for one minute. Drizzle over pork.

Serves 4

BEETS WITH DILL SAUCE

ALLISON MAY
SEATTLE, WA

We love this dish...it is so beautiful as well as yummy!

6 to 8 medium beets,
  cooked and peeled
1 lemon
1 T. olive oil
1 c. plain whole-milk
  yogurt
1 T. sour cream
1 t. sea salt
3 T. fresh dill, chopped
coarse pepper to taste

1 Cut the beets into wedges and arrange on a platter. Grate the zest off the lemon and set aside. Cut the lemon into wedges. Drizzle the beets with olive oil and squeeze the fresh lemon on them. In a small bowl, whisk together the yogurt, sour cream, salt and lemon zest. Drizzle the mixture on the beets. Sprinkle with dill; season with pepper.

Serves 4

COUNTRY KITCHEN
BEEF & VEGETABLES

MARY JO HANSON
CENTERVILLE, WA

This recipe came about using a little creativity and some leftovers. Now, it's a regular request at our house!

1 Brown beef with mushrooms and onions in olive oil and red wine in a Dutch oven; add remaining ingredients except noodles and butter.

2 Bring to a boil; reduce heat and simmer for one hour. To serve, toss noodles with butter; spoon beef mixture over noodles.

Serves 6 to 8

1-1/2 lbs. stew beef cubes

1-lb. pkg. sliced mushrooms

1 c. green onions, sliced

2 T. olive oil

1/4 c. red wine or beef broth

1-1/2 c. beef broth

1 T. garlic, minced

6-oz. can tomato paste

1/2 t. dried parsley

1/2 t. dried thyme

14-1/2 oz. can diced tomatoes

salt and pepper to taste

16-oz. pkg. egg noodles, cooked

2 T. butter, melted

COUNTRY POTATO CAKES

**CARLY ST. CLAIR
LYNNWOOD, WA**

*My grandmother used to make these with leftover mashed
potatoes and they were so delicious. Her secret was a
well-seasoned cast-iron skillet which gives a nice flavor and
aids in even browning. Great with meals any time of day!*

2 eggs, beaten
1/2 t. salt
1/4 t. pepper
3 c. mashed potatoes
1/2 c. all-purpose flour
1/2 c. green onions, diced
1/2 c. shredded Cheddar
  Jack cheese
canola oil for frying

1 In a bowl, whisk eggs with salt and pepper. Stir
in remaining ingredients except oil; set aside.
Meanwhile, add one inch oil to a cast-iron skillet
over medium-high heat. Heat until oil is very hot but
not smoking, about 375 degrees.

2 Add potato mixture to oil by 1/2 cupfuls. Cook until
golden on the bottom. With a spatula, turn potato
cakes over and flatten. Cook until golden on other
side. Drain on paper towels; serve hot.

Makes 6 to 8 servings

CREAMY BACON & HERB SUCCOTASH

VICKIE
GOOSEBERRY PATCH

You'll love this deluxe version of an old harvest-time favorite...I do!

1 Cook bacon until crisp in a Dutch oven over medium-high heat. Remove bacon, reserving 2 tablespoons drippings in Dutch oven. Add onion; sauté about 5 minutes, or until tender. Add beans, water, salt and pepper; bring to a boil.

2 Reduce heat; cover and simmer 5 minutes. Stir in corn, whipping cream and thyme; return to a simmer. Cook until vegetables are tender, about 5 minutes. Toss with bacon and chives before serving.

Serves 6

1/4 lb. bacon, chopped

1 onion, diced

10-oz. pkg. frozen lima beans

1/2 c. water

salt and pepper to taste

10-oz. pkg. frozen corn

1/2 c. whipping cream

1-1/2 t. fresh thyme, minced

Garnish: 2 t. fresh chives, snipped

WASHINGTON WONDERS

The so-called Cadillac of salmon is Copper River Salmon, which is flown in from Alaska in late spring. Big seafood restaurants vie to see who can get it first. It makes for a delicious but pricey meal. Supermarkets are in the mix, too, selling the delicacy for $40 to $50 per pound.

CHICKEN & SNOW PEA STIR-FRY

JENNIE GIST
GOOSEBERRY PATCH

Delicious! Also try this recipe with beef sirloin instead of chicken, diced fresh tomatoes and even Japanese-style buckwheat noodles. Quick and satisfying.

8-oz. pkg. medium egg noodles, uncooked

3/4 c. orange juice

3 T. low-sodium soy sauce

4 t. cornstarch

1 T. brown sugar, packed

1/2 t. ground ginger

1 lb. boneless, skinless chicken breast, thinly sliced

2 t. canola oil

14-1/2-oz. can diced tomatoes

2 c. snow peas, trimmed

1 Cook noodles according to package directions; drain. Meanwhile, in a small bowl, combine orange juice, soy sauce, cornstarch, brown sugar and ginger; mix well and set aside.

2 In a wok or large skillet over medium-high heat, cook and stir chicken in oil for 2 minutes, or until golden. Drain; add orange juice mixture and tomatoes with juice to skillet. Cook and stir until mixture is thickened. Add snow peas; cook and stir for 2 minutes, or until crisp-tender. Serve chicken mixture over hot noodles.

Makes 4 servings

EASY GARLIC-PARMESAN CHICKEN

DENISE ALLISON
GIG HARBOR, WA

My handy tip...for easy clean-up, line the pan with aluminum foil before spraying it with non-stick vegetable spray.

1 Mix mayonnaise, cheese and seasonings in a shallow bowl. Coat chicken breasts with mixture; cover with bread crumbs.

2 Arrange in a 13"x9" baking pan that has been sprayed with non-stick vegetable spray. Bake, uncovered, at 425 degrees for 20 to 25 minutes, until golden and chicken juices run clear.

Serves 4 to 6

3/4 c. mayonnaise
1/2 c. grated Parmesan cheese
1 t. garlic powder
1 t. Italian seasoning
4 to 6 boneless, skinless chicken breasts
1 c. Italian-flavored dry bread crumbs

DUCHESS DOGS

LOIS LONG-CRANE
KINGSTON, WA

My mom used to make this dish, and my sons loved it when they were growing up. From the list of simple ingredients, you'd never guess how good it is!

1 In a saucepan over medium heat, sauté onion in butter. Add boiling water to pan; remove from heat. Add milk; stir in potato flakes. Cool slightly; stir egg into potatoes. Meanwhile, simmer hot dogs in a saucepan of boiling water until heated through. Put hot dogs in a lightly greased 13"x9" baking pan and partially split them lengthwise. Spoon mashed potatoes evenly into hot dogs; sprinkle with cheese. Bake, uncovered, at 350 degrees for about 15 minutes, until cheese is melted.

Serves 4 to 8

1/2 c. onion, diced
5 T. butter
3 c. boiling water
1-1/4 c. cold milk
8-oz. pkg. instant mashed potato flakes
1 egg, beaten
1 lb. all-beef hot dogs
1/2 c. shredded Cheddar cheese

ROSEMARY PORK & MUSHROOMS

VICKIE
GOOSEBERRY PATCH

This simple dish is delicious with ordinary button mushrooms, but for a special dinner I'll use a combination of wild mushrooms...their earthy flavor goes so well with the fresh rosemary.

1 lb. pork tenderloin, cut
  into 8 slices
1 T. butter
1 c. sliced mushrooms
2 T. onion, finely
  chopped
1 clove garlic, minced
1 t. fresh rosemary,
  chopped
1/4 t. celery salt
1 T. sherry or apple
  juice

1 Flatten each pork slice to one-inch thick; set aside. Melt butter in a large skillet over medium-high heat. Cook pork slices just until golden, about one minute per side. Remove pork slices to a plate, reserving drippings in skillet. Add remaining ingredients except sherry or apple juice to skillet.

2 Reduce heat to low; cook for 2 minutes, stirring frequently. Stir in sherry or juice. Return pork slices to skillet; spoon mushroom mixture over top. Cover and simmer for 3 to 4 minutes, until the pork juices run clear. Serve pork slices topped with mushroom mixture.

Makes 4 servings, 2 slices each

FRUITED ROAST PORK

MELODY TAYNOR
EVERETT, WA

*I was looking for something just a little different to serve for
Christmas dinner...I'm glad I found this easy and delicious recipe!*

1 Place onion slices in the bottom of a slow cooker.
Add roast; top with fruit. Mix remaining ingredients in
a cup; drizzle over roast.

2 Cover and cook on low setting for 6 to 8 hours, until
pork is tender. Remove roast to a serving platter; let
stand several minutes before slicing. Serve sliced
roast topped with fruit sauce from slow cooker.

Serves 6 to 8

1 onion, sliced

2-lb. boneless pork loin
roast

7-oz. pkg. mixed dried
fruit, coarsely chopped

3/4 c. apple cider

1/2 t. nutmeg

1/4 t. cinnamon

1/2 t. salt

FRENCH RICE

MICHELLE LOCKETT
LEBAM, WA

An easy side dish to pop in the oven...who needs a boxed mix?

1 Combine all ingredients in a lightly greased
2-quart casserole dish. Stir gently. Cover and bake
at 350 degrees for 35 minutes, or until liquid is
absorbed and rice is tender.

Makes 4 to 5 servings

1 c. long-cooking rice,
uncooked

4-oz. can sliced
mushrooms, drained

1/2 c. onion, chopped

10-1/2 oz. can French
onion soup

1 c. beef consommé

1/2 c. butter, melted

1/3 c. water

1 T. fresh parsley,
chopped

1 clove garlic, minced

GINGER-LIME GRILLED SALMON

JO ANN
GOOSEBERRY PATCH

Serve this delicious dish with a spinach salad made using sliced tomatoes and cucumbers for a complete meal.

2 T. butter, melted
2 T. fresh ginger, peeled and minced
2 T. lime zest
1 T. lime juice
1/2 t. salt
1/2 t. pepper
2 lbs. salmon fillets, 1-inch thick
Garnish: lime wedges

1 In a small bowl, combine all ingredients except salmon and garnish. Rub mixture over salmon fillets.

2 Place fish on a lightly oiled grate over medium-high heat. Cover and grill salmon about 5 minutes on each side, until fish flakes easily with a fork. Garnish with lime wedges.

Serves 4 to 6

SCOTTISH SHEPHERD'S PIE

VICKI SHEARER
RENTON, WA

My Scottish husband loves this casserole...it smells so yummy baking on a cold winter's night. I like to use leftover mashed potatoes but, in a pinch, instant potatoes will do.

1 lb. lean ground beef
1/2 c. yellow onion, diced
1 c. carrot, peeled and diced
1-oz. pkg. brown gravy mix
1 to 3 t. curry powder, to taste
4 c. mashed potatoes, warmed

1 Brown beef, onion and carrot in a skillet over medium heat; drain. Meanwhile, prepare gravy mix according to package directions; stir desired amount of curry powder into gravy. Add gravy to beef mixture.

2 Spoon into an ungreased 2-quart casserole dish. Top with warm mashed potatoes. Bake, uncovered, at 350 degrees for 30 to 35 minutes.

Makes 4 to 6 servings

GRANDMA'S SLOW-COOKED BAKED BEANS

TINA HENGEN
CLARKSTON, WA

Whenever I travelled to visit my grandmother, she would always have something hot and delicious ready to serve. This was one of my most favorites...it's scrumptious!

1 In a large saucepan, cover beans with water. Bring to a boil over high heat; boil for 2 minutes. Cover pan and let stand for one hour.

2 Drain and rinse beans; transfer to a slow cooker. Stir in 3-1/2 cups fresh water and remaining ingredients except salt. Cover and cook on low setting for 10 to 12 hours. Season with salt.

Serves 10 to 12

1 lb. dried navy beans
3-1/2 c. water
1 onion, chopped
4 slices bacon, chopped
1/4 c. molasses
2 t. dry mustard
1/4 t. pepper
1/8 t. ground cloves
salt to taste

HAND-ME-DOWN BROCCOLI SOUFFLÉ

LACEY WAHL
PORT TOWNSEND, WA

This recipe has been handed down through my family, and it's a must at any holiday.

1 Combine all ingredients except garnish in a lightly greased 2-quart casserole dish. Mix well.

2 Bake, uncovered, at 350 degrees for about 30 minutes. Garnish as desired; return to oven for 5 minutes.

Serves 6 to 8

2 10-oz. pkgs. frozen chopped broccoli, thawed and drained
10-3/4 oz. can cream of mushroom soup
2 eggs, beaten
1 c. mayonnaise
1 c. shredded Cheddar cheese
1/2 c. onion, finely chopped
Garnish: additional cheese and/or canned French fried onions

HAMBURGER PIE

MARIE BUCHE
YAKIMA, WA

With a family of six on a ministry budget, this easy, affordable recipe became the first dinner I taught my three daughters and my son to prepare. Even the leftovers are tasty. This is also my most-requested church potluck recipe. Serve with cinnamon-spiced applesauce for a wonderful family dinner.

2 lbs. ground beef

1 onion, chopped

2 10-3/4 oz. cans tomato soup

28-oz. can green beans, drained

salt and pepper to taste

1 c. shredded Cheddar cheese

1 Brown beef and onion together in a skillet; drain. Mix soup and beans in a lightly greased 13"x9" baking pan. Stir in beef mixture, salt and pepper; set aside.

2 Spread Potato Topping evenly over mixture in pan; sprinkle with cheese. Bake, uncovered, at 350 degrees for about 30 minutes.

Makes 12 servings

POTATO TOPPING:

3 c. milk

3 c. water

1/4 c. margarine

1 t. salt

4 c. instant mashed potato flakes

1 Bring all ingredients except potato flakes to a boil. Stir in potato flakes; mix well. Cover and let stand for 5 minutes. If potatoes are too thick to spread, add milk or water to desired consistency.

SAUSAGE & RICE CASSEROLE

LIZ WATANABE
KENT, WA

My mom has made this yummy casserole for several years. I always thought it must be very complicated because it was so delicious. One night we were having dinner at Mom & Dad's. My husband found out how good it is and I had no choice but to try making it myself! It's comfort food that's very easy to prepare, and yet scrumptious enough to serve to guests.

1 In a large, deep skillet over medium heat, cook sausage, onion and celery, stirring often to break up sausage. Drain, reserving 1-1/2 tablespoons drippings in skillet with sausage mixture. Add pepper and set aside.

2 Meanwhile, in a very large stockpot over high heat, bring water to a boil. Add uncooked rice and soup mix to boiling water; stir well and add sausage mixture. Stir to mix completely; mixture will be very watery. Transfer to a greased deep 3-quart casserole dish.

3 Bake, uncovered, at 350 degrees for 20 minutes. Remove from oven; stir. Cover and bake an additional 30 to 40 minutes, until liquid is absorbed and rice is tender.

Makes 10 to 12 servings

2 lbs. ground pork
   sausage
1 onion, chopped
3 to 4 c. celery, chopped
1/8 t. pepper, or to taste
9 c. water
2 c. long-cooking rice,
   uncooked
3 2-oz. envs. chicken
   noodle soup mix,
   uncooked

HERBED MASHED POTATOES

VICKIE
GOOSEBERRY PATCH

*Filled with fresh herbs, these potatoes are just wonderful! Serve
topped with a large pat of melting butter, of course.*

**6-1/2 c. potatoes, peeled
and cubed**
2 cloves garlic, halved
1/2 c. milk
1/2 c. sour cream
1 T. butter, softened
**2 T. fresh oregano,
minced**
**1 T. fresh parsley,
minced**
1 T. fresh thyme, minced
3/4 t. salt
1/8 t. pepper

1 Place potatoes and garlic in a large saucepan;
cover potatoes with water. Bring to a boil over
medium high heat.

2 Reduce heat to medium; simmer for
20 minutes, or until potatoes are very tender.
Drain; return potatoes and garlic to pan. Add
remaining ingredients; beat with an electric mixer
at medium speed to desired consistency.

Serves 6 to 8

ITALIAN BREAD CRUMBS

MELODY TAYNOR
EVERETT, WA

This is thrifty twice...use up leftover bread and save on store-bought bread crumbs at the same time! I keep bread in the freezer until I have enough slices. The seasoned bread crumbs can be added directly to a recipe without thawing, or thaw them briefly at room temperature.

1 Place bread on a baking sheet and bake at 300 degrees for about 15 minutes, until dried out. Tear slices into pieces and process to fine crumbs in a food processor. Add remaining ingredients; process until combined. Place in a freezer-safe container; keep frozen.

Makes about 4 cups

12 slices bread
1 t. dried parsley
1 t. garlic powder
1 t. onion powder
1 t. sugar
1 t. salt
1/2 t. pepper
1/2 t. Italian seasoning

SAUSAGE CRESCENT ROLLS

DANA ROWAN
SPOKANE, WA

I have a teenage son who is always hungry! When his friends come over, they devour everything in my pantry. I learned that tucking pretty much any filling (even leftover casserole) into a crescent roll is a quick, inexpensive way to feed a lot of people. This recipe is so easy and delicious!

1 Lightly brown sausage in a skillet over medium heat; drain. While sausage is still hot, add cream cheese. Stir until cheese is melted and mixture is creamy. Remove from heat; cool completely. Unroll crescent rolls; arrange into 2 rectangles.

2 Form a log of sausage mixture lengthwise down the center of each rectangle. Fold over the long sides to cover each sausage log. Place rolls seam-side down on an ungreased baking sheet. Brush with egg white. Bake at 350 degrees for 20 minutes, or until crust is golden. Allow to cool completely; slice one to 1-1/2 inches thick.

Makes 10 to 20 pieces

1 lb. mild or spicy ground pork breakfast sausage
8-oz. pkg. cream cheese, softened
2 8-oz. tubes refrigerated crescent rolls
1 egg white, lightly beaten

KIMBERLY'S CREAMY BEEF & POTATOES

KIMBERLY ADAMS
TACOMA, WA

My favorite one-pot meal.

1 lb. ground beef,
  browned and drained
8 potatoes, peeled and
  thinly sliced
1 c. frozen sliced carrots
1/2 onion, minced
10-3/4 oz. can cream of
  mushroom soup
10-3/4 oz. can broccoli
  cheese soup
1 c. milk
1 t. salt

1 Place browned beef into a slow cooker; add potatoes, carrots and onion. Stir together remaining ingredients; pour over top. Cover and cook on low setting for 7 to 8 hours.

Makes 6 to 8 servings

SKILLET BBQ PORK CHOPS

CAROL HUMMEL
KIRKLAND, WA

I've been making these savory, tender pork chops for years...comfort food at its finest!

1 T. oil
4 to 6 pork chops
1/3 c. celery, chopped
2 T. brown sugar,
  packed
2 T. lemon juice
1-1/2 t. dry mustard
1-1/2 t. salt
1/8 t. pepper
2 8-oz. cans tomato
  sauce

1 Heat oil in a large skillet over medium heat. Brown pork chops on both sides; drain. Sprinkle celery, brown sugar, lemon juice and seasonings evenly over pork chops.

2 Spoon tomato sauce over all. Cover and simmer over low heat for one hour.

Serves 4 to 6

KRISTIN'S SWEET & TANGY GREEN BEANS

LISA KASTNING
MARYSVILLE, WA

My friend Kristin shared this recipe with me over 20 years ago, and it's still one of my favorite ways to eat green beans. I've never tasted anything like them...hope you enjoy them too!

1 Add green beans with liquid to a saucepan. Heat over low heat until warmed through; drain. Meanwhile, in a skillet over medium heat, sauté mushrooms and onion in butter until tender, 5 to 7 minutes. Stir in water chestnuts.

2 In a bowl, whisk together sour cream and remaining ingredients; add to mushroom mixture and warm through. Pour over warmed green beans. Stir gently and serve.

Serves 6

2 15-oz. cans French-cut green beans
1 c. sliced mushrooms
1/2 c. onion, diced
2 T. butter, sliced
8-oz. can water chestnuts, drained and chopped
1 c. sour cream
1 t. sugar
1 t. salt
1 t. vinegar

LEMONY PORK PICCATA

MELODY TAYNOR
EVERETT, WA

*Serve over quick-cooking angel hair pasta to enjoy every drop of
the lemony sauce.*

1-lb. pork tenderloin,
  sliced into 8 portions
2 t. lemon-pepper
  seasoning
3 T. all-purpose flour
2 T. butter, divided
1/4 c. dry sherry or
  chicken broth
1/4 c. lemon juice
1/4 c. capers
4 to 6 thin slices lemon

1 Pound pork slices to 1/8-inch thickness, using a meat mallet or rolling pin. Lightly sprinkle pork with seasoning and flour.

2 Melt one tablespoon butter in a large skillet over medium-high heat. Add half of pork and sauté for 2 to 3 minutes on each side, until golden, turning once. Remove pork to a serving plate; set aside.

3 Repeat with remaining butter and pork. Add sherry or chicken broth, lemon juice, capers and lemon slices to skillet. Cook for 2 minutes or until slightly thickened, scraping up browned bits. Add pork and heat through.

Serves 4

Herbed Mashed
Potatoes, p. 76

Whether you are looking for a quick-to-make breakfast dish to start the day off right, no-fuss party fare for those special guests, satisfying soups and sandwiches for the perfect lunch, main dishes to bring them to the table fast, or a sweet little something to savor at the end of the meal, you'll love these recipes from the amazing cooks in beautiful Washington State.

Cherry Berry Chocolate
Cake, p. 125

Pepper Steak Sammies, p. 31

All-American Sandwiches, p. 26

Apple & Brie Toasts, p. 111

Mac & Cheese Nuggets, p. 113

Chilled Apple &
Cheese Salad, p. 32

Apple Blush Pie, p. 122

Spinach & Provolone-Stuffed
Chicken, p. 51

Cheesy Spinach-Stuffed
Mushrooms, p. 103

Famous Blueberry Cake, p. 138

Checkerboard Cheese
Sandwiches, p. 108

Chinese Coleslaw, p. 35

Cream Cheese Terrine, p. 107

Creamy Bacon &
Herb Succotash, p. 67

Chocolate-Berry Trifles, p. 136

Colby Corn Chowder, p. 36

Tangy Deviled Eggs, p. 106

Foil-Wrapped Baked Salmon, p. 96

Cherry Tomato Hummus Wraps, p. 32

Beets with Dill Sauce, p. 64

LOLITA'S CHICKEN ADOBO

ANGELA VINING
TACOMA, WA

*This recipe was passed down by my husband's Filipino cousin
and is a family favorite. It's just as good if you use pork instead of
chicken! You can find coconut vinegar in the Asian food section of
your grocery store.*

1 Arrange chicken pieces in a slow cooker; set
aside. Combine vinegar, soy sauce, garlic and
spices in a bowl; drizzle over chicken.

2 Cover and cook on low setting for 6 to 8 hours,
until chicken is no longer pink in the center. Shred
chicken, discarding bones; return to sauce in slow
cooker. Discard bay leaves before serving. Serve
chicken and sauce over rice.

Serves 8

4 to 5 lbs. chicken
2 c. coconut vinegar
1/2 c. soy sauce
1 clove garlic, pressed
1-1/2 T. pepper
10 bay leaves
cooked rice

SPEEDY BAKED BEANS

MARI BOCHENEK
LACEY, WA

*This recipe is amazing! It only takes 10 minutes in the microwave,
yet the beans taste like they've been slow-baked for hours.*

1 Stir together all ingredients in a microwave-safe
casserole dish. Cover; microwave on high for
10 minutes. Stir again and serve.

Makes 6 to 10 servings

16-oz. pkg. bacon, crisply
   cooked and crumbled
2 15-oz. cans pork &
   beans
1 onion, finely chopped
1/4 c. brown sugar,
   packed
1/4 c. maple syrup
1/4 c. catsup
1/2 t. dry mustard
1/4 to 1/2 t. cayenne
   pepper

MAPLE POT ROAST

LISA WINDHORN
SEATTLE, WA

Just as tasty made in the slow cooker. Cook on low setting for 8 to 10 hours, or on high setting for 4 to 6 hours.

2-lb. boneless beef chuck roast

1/2 c. orange juice

1/2 c. maple syrup

2 T. red wine vinegar

1 T. Worcestershire sauce

2 t. orange zest

1/4 t. salt

1/4 t. pepper

2 carrots, peeled and cut into 2-inch pieces

2 stalks celery, cut into 2-inch pieces

1 onion, chopped

2 potatoes, peeled and cut into 2-inch cubes

1 Brown roast over medium heat in a Dutch oven sprayed with non-stick vegetable spray.

2 In a bowl, combine orange juice, syrup, vinegar, Worcestershire sauce, orange zest, salt and pepper. Pour over roast. Bring to a boil. Reduce heat; cover and simmer one hour. Add carrots, celery and onions; cover and simmer 20 minutes. Add potatoes; cover and simmer for 20 minutes, until tender.

Makes 4 to 6 servings

MOM'S PIZZA LOAF

**LINDA THOMAS
EVERETT, WA**

My mom has made this recipe for as long as I can remember...it was a Saturday night tradition in my family.

1 Combine uncooked meat, Parmesan cheese, olives, onion, tomato paste and seasonings; mix well. Spread evenly on each half of loaf, making sure to spread to edges.

2 Place both halves on an ungreased baking sheet. Broil about 5 inches from heat for about 12 minutes, or until meat is done. Top with tomato and cheese slices. Return to broiler for one to 2 minutes, just until cheese begins to melt. Slice into serving-size pieces.

Serves 8

1 to 1-1/2 lbs. ground beef or turkey

1/2 c. grated Parmesan cheese

1/3 c. green olives with pimentos, chopped

1/3 c. onion, chopped

2 6-oz. cans tomato paste

1 t. garlic powder

3/4 t. dried oregano

1 t. salt

1 loaf French bread, halved lengthwise

3 tomatoes, thinly sliced

1 lb. sliced Cheddar cheese

GOOD FOR YOU

Choose whole-grain breads, pita rounds or flatbreads to make your recipes a bit more nutritious. You'll love the taste and texture and it is good for you.

MOM'S SKILLET SWISS STEAK

**ANETT YEAGER
LA CENTER, WA**

*My mom used to make this weekly...now my family asks for it often.
I serve it with mashed potatoes and a green salad...a real comfort
food meal!*

1 lb. beef sirloin tip
steak or bottom round
steak
3 T. all-purpose flour
3 T. butter
2 8-oz. cans tomato
sauce
1 T. Worcestershire
sauce
1 T. soy sauce
1 T. lemon juice
1 onion, sliced
1 green pepper, sliced
cooked rice or noodles

1 Thinly slice beef across the grain into strips.
Lightly coat beef with flour.

2 Melt butter in a large skillet over medium heat;
brown beef, one-half at a time. Return all beef to
skillet. Add sauces and lemon juice; mix well. Add
onion and green pepper.

3 Cover and simmer for 45 minutes, or until beef
is tender, stirring occasionally. Serve over rice or
noodles.

Serves 4

WASHINGTON WONDERS

To get a hint of how Washington residents love to
celebrate food, simply visit one of its main tourist
attractions and destination spots, Pike Place Market.
Be ready to duck, as workers toss whole fish across the
counter. It's Seattle's original farmers' market, and you'll
marvel at the character of the place. Savor the sights,
sounds and aromas. Grab a snack or lunch at one of the
many spots inside the market, established in 1907.

MUSTARD & THYME POTATO SALAD

CINDE SHIELDS
ISSAQUAH, WA

One creamy bite of potato salad brings back cherished memories of family reunions in the park, summertime pool parties and my grandmother's busy kitchen.

1 Pierce potatoes with a fork; bake at 400 degrees for 45 minutes, or until tender. When still warm but cool enough to handle, remove and discard skins. Cut into bite-size pieces.

2 Transfer potatoes to a medium glass bowl. While potatoes are still warm, lightly drizzle with vinegar. Fold potatoes over and lightly drizzle again. Gently fold once more; set aside. In a small bowl, combine mayonnaise, mustard, thyme and pepper. Pour over potatoes. Fold until evenly coated. Transfer to a serving bowl; garnish with thyme. Serve warm or chilled.

Serves 4 to 6

2 baking potatoes
1 to 2 T. red wine vinegar, divided
1 c. mayonnaise
2 T. plus 2 t. Dijon mustard
1 t. fresh thyme, minced, or 1/2 t. dried thyme
pepper to taste
Garnish: 2 sprigs fresh thyme

MOM'S BROCCOLI CASSEROLE

**HEATHER ALEXANDER
LACEY, WA**

Our holidays wouldn't be complete without this dish!

2 10-oz. pkg's. chopped broccoli

2 T. onion, minced

5 T. butter, divided

3 T. all-purpose flour

1-1/2 c. milk

2 t. salt

1/4 t. pepper

3 eggs, hard-boiled, peeled and chopped

1/2 c. shredded Cheddar cheese

1/2 c. corn flake cereal, crushed

1 Prepare broccoli as directed on package; set aside. Sauté onion in 3 tablespoons butter until tender; stir in flour. Add milk, salt and pepper; bring to a boil, stirring often.

2 Remove from heat; set aside. Place broccoli in a greased 13"x9" baking pan; sprinkle with eggs. Pour milk mixture over the top; stir well and set aside.

3 Melt remaining butter; combine with cheese and cereal. Crumble over broccoli mixture; bake at 375 degrees for 20 minutes.

Serves 8

OH-SO-EASY LASAGNA

JO ANN
GOOSEBERRY PATCH

This recipe is so easy to customize with what you have on hand. Really, any flavor pasta sauce will work, and feel free to try it with ground turkey or pork if you like.

1 Mix together ground beef and pasta sauce. In a slow cooker, layer half each of ground beef mixture, pasta, cottage cheese and shredded cheese. Repeat with remaining ingredients. Cover and cook on low setting for 6 to 8 hours, or on high setting for 3 to 4 hours.

Serves 8

1 to 2 lbs. ground beef, browned and drained

26-oz. jar Parmesan & Romano pasta sauce

8-oz. pkg. bowtie pasta, cooked

12-oz. container cottage cheese

16-oz. pkg. shredded mozzarella cheese

VEGGIES ON THE GRILL

SANDRA COMMINS
KENNEWICK, WA

My husband sells onions for a large farm here in Washington. This recipe is one of his favorites. Just put it on the grill alongside the meat you're grilling for dinner.

1 Coat a 14-inch length of heavy-duty aluminum foil with non-stick vegetable spray. Layer vegetables on foil. Pour dressing over all; sprinkle with seasoning. Seal foil packet.

2 Grill over medium heat for about 25 to 30 minutes, until crisp-tender. May also bake packet on a baking pan at 350 degrees for about 30 minutes.

Serves 4

1 sweet or mild onion, cut into large chunks

1 green or red pepper, cut into squares

1/2 lb. sliced mushrooms

1/2 c. sun-dried tomato vinaigrette salad dressing

1/2 t. Italian seasoning

ONSIDE KICKIN' CHICKEN KABOBS

MELODY TAYNOR
EVERETT, WA

I made these for a tailgating party one time and they were a huge hit. Turns out that our team ended up winning the game with a recovered onside kick, so I just had to name this recipe in their honor!

2 T. olive oil
2 T. fresh cilantro, chopped
juice of one lime
1 t. ground cumin
salt and pepper to taste
2 boneless, skinless chicken breasts, cubed
1 zucchini, sliced
1 onion, cut into wedges
1 red pepper, cut into 1-inch pieces
10 cherry tomatoes

1 In a bowl, combine oil, cilantro, lime juice and seasonings. Add chicken; stir to mix well. Cover and refrigerate for at least one hour.

2 Thread chicken, zucchini, onion, red pepper and tomatoes onto skewers. Grill skewers over high heat, turning occasionally, for about 10 minutes, or until chicken is no longer pink in the center.

Makes 4

YUMMY POTATO TOPPING

KATHLEEN POPP
OAK HARBOR, WA

Spoon this topping onto baked potatoes...scrumptious!

1/2 c. butter, softened
3/4 c. sour cream
1 c. shredded Cheddar cheese

1 Blend butter, sour cream and cheese together. Use immediately or keep refrigerated.

Makes 4 servings

PAMELA'S GARLIC BREAD

**PAMELA DELACRUZ
MOUNT VERNON, WA**

For a time, we attended church services in the home of a friend, followed by a meal together. This bread was often requested...it was always snatched up as soon as it was cool enough to eat!

1 In a bowl, combine all ingredients except bread; mix until well blended.

2 Evenly spread mixture on bread halves. Place on an ungreased baking sheet. Bake at 350 degrees for 10 to 15 minutes. Let cool and slice.

Makes 12 servings

8-oz. pkg. cream cheese, softened
4-oz. can chopped black olives, drained
4 green onions, chopped
2 to 3 cloves garlic, finely chopped
1/4 c. Italian seasoning
1/4 c. butter, softened
1 loaf French bread, halved lengthwise

EASY FANCY BROCCOLI

**JO ANN
GOOSEBERRY PATCH**

What an easy dish to make and it tastes delightful!

1 Toast pine nuts in a large skillet over medium heat 6 minutes, or until golden. Remove from skillet and set aside. Heat butter and oil in same skillet over medium heat until butter melts. Add garlic; sauté one to 2 minutes, or until golden. Add broccoli, salt and red pepper flakes. Sauté 8 minutes, or until broccoli is tender. Stir in pine nuts before serving.

Makes 6 servings

2 T. pine nuts
1 T. butter
1 T. olive oil
6 cloves garlic, thinly sliced
1 lb. broccoli flowerets
1/8 t. salt
1/8 t. red pepper flakes

FOIL-WRAPPED BAKED SALMON

JO ANN
GOOSEBERRY PATCH

This is such an easy recipe, and it always turns out to be everyone's favorite!

4 salmon fillets
1 onion, sliced
1/4 c. butter, diced
1 lemon, thinly sliced
1/4 c. brown sugar, packed

1 Place each fillet on a piece of aluminum foil that has been sprayed with non-stick vegetable spray. Top fillets evenly with onion slices, diced butter, lemon slices and brown sugar.

2 Fold over foil tightly to make packets; make several holes in top of packets with a fork to allow steam to escape. Arrange packets on an ungreased baking sheet. Bake at 375 degrees for 15 to 20 minutes.

Serves 4

GOOD FOR YOU

Salmon is one of the healthiest proteins you can choose. This health-supportive food is unusually high in omega-3 fatty acid content, and it is also high in all kinds of nutrients including vitamin B-12.

PARMESAN MEATBALLS

JUDITH LEVY
SUMNER, WA

My mother gave me this delicious recipe over 50 years ago when I was first married. Everyone at our open houses raves about it. It's an easy make-ahead since the meatballs and sauce can be frozen.

1 In a large bowl, combine beef, bread crumbs, milk, egg, cheese, onion, salt and pepper. Mix well; form into 1/2-inch meatballs.

2 Melt butter in a large skillet over medium heat. Add meatballs; brown on all sides. Remove meatballs to a plate. Add flour to drippings in skillet; blend well. Add undrained mushrooms and remaining ingredients to skillet. Cook, stirring constantly, until thickened and smooth. Season with salt and pepper. Add meatballs to sauce in skillet; cover and simmer for 20 minutes.

Serves 20

1 lb. ground beef
1/2 c. dry bread crumbs
1/2 c. milk
1 egg, lightly beaten
1/2 c. grated Parmesan cheese
1 T. dried, minced onion
salt and pepper to taste
2 T. butter, sliced
1/4 c. all-purpose flour
4-oz. can mushroom stems & pieces
1 c. canned beef consommé or broth
1/2 c. sauterne wine or water
1/2 c. light cream

PARMESAN POTATOES

GRETCHEN MORTLOCK
VANCOUVER, WA

I often make these savory potatoes when we have guests for dinner...they're always enjoyed!

5 lbs. russet potatoes, peeled and sliced 1/4-inch thick
3 t. salt, divided
1/2 t. pepper
1-1/2 T. fresh rosemary, minced
3/4 c. crumbled blue cheese
1-1/2 c. shredded Parmesan cheese, divided
1 c. sour cream
2 c. whipping cream

1 In a large bowl, toss potatoes with 2 teaspoons salt, pepper and rosemary. Layer half of the potatoes in a buttered 13"x9" baking pan.

2 In a small bowl, toss blue cheese and 3/4 cup Parmesan cheese together. Sprinkle half of cheese mixture over potatoes.

3 In a separate bowl, whisk together sour cream, whipping cream and remaining salt. Pour cream mixture over potatoes. Tap baking pan gently to release any air bubbles. Sprinkle with remaining cheese mixture; top with remaining Parmesan cheese. Bake, uncovered, at 350 degrees for one hour and 30 minutes, or until golden and potatoes are tender.

Makes 8 servings

PEPPERONI-PIZZA RIGATONI

JO ANN
GOOSEBERRY PATCH

Personalize this recipe by adding mushrooms, black olives or any of your family's other favorite pizza toppings.

1 Alternate layers of ground beef, cooked rigatoni, cheese, soup, sauce and pepperoni in a slow cooker. Cover and cook on low setting for 4 hours.

Serves 6

1-1/2 lbs. ground beef, browned

8-oz. pkg. rigatoni, cooked

16-oz. pkg. shredded mozzarella cheese

10-3/4 oz. can cream of tomato soup

2 14-oz. jars pizza sauce

8-oz. pkg. sliced pepperoni

HEALTHY FACT

Parsley is an herb that can be used in so many ways. Used fresh, it makes a lovely garnish. In breads, soups and other recipes it adds flavor, color, and Vitamins K, C and A.

CHAPTER FOUR

NO-FUSS

Appetizers

WHETHER YOU ARE HAVING

A SPECIAL PARTY OR JUST

NEED A LITTLE SNACK TO TIDE

YOU OVER TO THE NEXT MEAL,

THESE LITTLE GOODIES ARE

SURE TO BECOME FAVORITE

GO-TO TREATS.

5-LAYER ITALIAN DIP

VICKI NELSON
PUYALLUP, WA

This dip is gone in no time! I can't tell you how many times I have shared this recipe. With the red and green colors used, it's especially nice around the holidays. If I take it to a potluck and the oven is being used, I just pop it in the microwave for about 5 minutes, and it turns out just as well. I like to use a quiche dish for a pretty presentation.

8-oz. container whipped
  cream cheese
1/4 c. grated Parmesan
  cheese
1/3 c. basil pesto sauce
1/2 c. roasted red
  peppers, drained and
  chopped
1 c. shredded mozzarella
  cheese
snack crackers or sliced
  Italian bread

1 In a bowl, blend together cream cheese and Parmesan cheese. Spread in the bottom of a 9" quiche dish or pie plate. Spread pesto sauce over cheese mixture. Sprinkle red peppers over pesto sauce. Sprinkle mozzarella cheese over the peppers.

2 Bake, uncovered, at 350 degrees for 15 minutes, or until heated through and cheeses are melted. Serve hot with crackers or Italian bread.

Serves 8

ANGEL EGGS

PAMELA DELACRUZ
MOUNT VERNON, WA

Deviled eggs are a favorite at our church gatherings, so I experiment with various ingredients looking for the yummy factor. So flavorful, yet it's so easy and there's no messy bowl to clean up...yay!

1 Arrange egg white halves on a platter; set aside. Combine egg yolks, cheese, mayonnaise or cream cheese and seasoning in a plastic zipping bag. Mash everything together until well blended. Cut off one small corner of bag; squeeze filling into egg whites. Garnish with bacon bits. Keep refrigerated.

Makes one dozen

6 eggs, hard-boiled, peeled and halved lengthwise
1/2 c. onion-flavored spreadable cream cheese
1/4 c. mayonnaise or cream cheese
1 t. Montreal steak seasoning
Garnish: bacon bits

CHEESY SPINACH-STUFFED MUSHROOMS

CINDE SHIELDS
ISSAQUAH, WA

This classic appetizer is always a hit, but this version is extra special because of the feta and cream cheese. Yummy!

1 In a bowl, combine all ingredients except mushroom caps and Parmesan cheese; mix well. Spoon mixture into mushrooms; place on a rimmed baking sheet.

2 Sprinkle mushrooms with Parmesan cheese. Bake at 350 degrees for 15 to 20 minutes, until bubbly and heated through. Serve warm.

Makes about 8 servings

10-oz. pkg. frozen chopped spinach, thawed and squeezed dry
1/4 c. cream cheese, softened
1 c. crumbled feta cheese
3/4 t. garlic powder
1/4 t. pepper
24 mushrooms, stems removed
1 c. grated Parmesan cheese

AVOCADO DIP

SUSIE ROGERS
PUYALLUP, WA

Add a bit of diced red onion or pimento for extra flavor and color!

2 avocados, pitted, peeled
  and chopped
8-oz. pkg. cream cheese,
  softened
1/4 c. mayonnaise
1/2 to 1 t. garlic salt

1 Blend all ingredients together; cover and chill until serving.

Makes about 2 cups

BECKY'S FAVORITE GLAZED WALNUTS

REBECCA JAHNKE
TRACYTON, WA

One day I found this among my grandmother's recipe cards and gave it a try. It was perfect for what I needed! Now it's a weakness for my friend Becky...my oldest daughter and I really like these nuts too. Their sweet simplicity has become a favorite!

1/2 c. butter, sliced
1 c. brown sugar, packed
1 t. cinnamon
4 c. walnut halves

1 Place butter in a microwave-safe 2-quart bowl. Microwave on high setting for one minute. Add brown sugar and cinnamon; microwave for 2 minutes.

2 Add walnut halves and toss to coat. Microwave for 5 minutes. Spread nuts on a baking sheet; allow to cool. Store in an airtight container.

Makes about 4 cups

HARVEST CIDER

VICKIE
GOOSEBERRY PATCH

*This spiced beverage will warm you up after football cheering,
trick-or-treating or just a brisk walk around the neighborhood
to savor the colorful autumn leaves.*

1 In a stockpot over medium-low heat, combine
frozen concentrates and water. Stir well as juices
melt. Add spices, enclosed in a muslin spice bag.
Bring to a boil.

2 Reduce heat to low; cover and simmer for
15 minutes. Discard spice bag; stir in schnapps,
if using. Pour into mugs; garnish with cinnamon
sticks for stirring.

Serves 12

12-oz. can frozen apple
juice concentrate

12-oz. can frozen
cranberry-apple juice
concentrate

6-oz. can frozen
lemonade concentrate

9 c. water

5 4-inch cinnamon
sticks

1 t. whole nutmeg,
coarsely chopped

7 whole cloves

Optional: 1/3 c.
cinnamon schnapps

Garnish: additional
cinnamon sticks

COMFORT-IN-A-MUG HOT CHOCOLATE

SAMANTHA REILLY
GIG HARBOR, WA

This is some of the richest, most chocolatey hot chocolate you'll ever sip. A mug of this treat is just what the doctor ordered after a long afternoon of leaf raking or a visit to the pumpkin patch!

14-oz. can sweetened
  condensed milk
7-1/2 c. water
1-1/2 t. vanilla extract
1/2 c. baking cocoa
1/8 t. salt
Garnish: marshmallows

1 Combine condensed milk, water and vanilla in a slow cooker; stir. Mix in cocoa and salt; stir until smooth. Cover and cook on high setting for 2 hours, or until heated through and smooth. Serve in mugs, topped with marshmallows.

Serves 8

TANGY DEVILED EGGS

JO ANN
GOOSEBERRY PATCH

No family reunion is complete without deviled eggs!

4 eggs, hard-boiled and
  peeled
1 t. prepared
  horseradish
1 t. onion, minced
1/3 c. light mayonnaise
1/4 t. celery salt
Garnish: sliced green
  onion

1 Slice eggs in half lengthwise and remove yolks. Mince yolks in a small mixing bowl; combine with horseradish, onion, mayonnaise and salt. Spoon mixture into egg white halves; keep chilled. Garnish as desired.

Makes 8 servings

CREAM CHEESE TERRINE

AMY PALSROCK
SILVERDALE, WA

My family & friends all call this my twenty-dollar dip...it looks (and tastes!) like it's from a gourmet store.

1 Blend one package cream cheese with garlic and herbes de Provence, if using; spread into a plastic wrap-lined 8"x4" loaf pan. Sprinkle with basil; chill for 15 minutes.

2 Mix second package cream cheese with tomatoes and onion; spread over first layer. Sprinkle with parsley; chill for 15 minutes.

3 Blend third package cream cheese with blue cheese and almonds; spread over tomato layer. Chill for 15 minutes. Combine remaining package cream cheese with pesto; spread over blue cheese layer. Cover and chill for at least one hour.

4 To serve, gently pull up on plastic wrap; invert onto a serving platter and peel away plastic wrap. Serve with crackers.

Serves 12

4 8-oz. pkgs. cream cheese, softened and divided

2 cloves garlic, chopped

Optional: 2 t. herbes de Provence

1/8 t. dried basil

7-oz. pkg. sun-dried tomatoes, sliced

3 T. green onion, sliced

1/8 t. dried parsley

4-oz. pkg. crumbled blue cheese

1/2 c. sliced almonds

7-oz. jar basil pesto sauce

assorted snack crackers

CREAMY SALMON ROLL-UPS

MELODY TAYNOR
EVERETT, WA

Gram used to make a version of this with canned salmon. Now I've jazzed it up with smoked salmon...delicious!

1-1/2 c. cream cheese, softened
4-oz. pkg. smoked salmon, chopped
3 T. capers, drained and chopped
1/4 c. fresh dill, chopped
4 10-inch flour tortillas

1 In a bowl, combine all ingredients except tortillas; blend well. Spread filling evenly over tortillas. Roll up tortillas tightly, jelly-roll fashion. Wrap each roll in plastic wrap.

2 Refrigerate 4 hours or overnight, until firm. Unwrap; trim ends of rolls and slice 1/2-inch thick.

Makes about 3-1/2 dozen

CHECKERBOARD CHEESE SANDWICHES

VICKIE
GOOSEBERRY PATCH

These dainty little sandwiches are always a must-have at our card club parties. Stack the sliced bread when you cut off the crusts and it will take less time.

2 c. shredded extra-sharp Cheddar cheese
2 c. shredded Swiss cheese
1 c. mayonnaise
4-oz. jar diced pimentos, drained
1 t. dried, minced onion
1/4 t. pepper
20 thin slices white bread, crusts trimmed
20 thin slices wheat bread, crusts trimmed

1 Stir together first 6 ingredients. Spread half of mixture on 10 white bread slices; top with remaining half of white bread slices. Spread remaining mixture on 10 wheat bread slices; top with remaining half of wheat bread slices.

2 Cut each sandwich into 4 squares. Arrange, stacked in pairs, in a pattern, alternating white and wheat.

Makes 40, serves 20

FARMHOUSE SALSA

DEBI HANSEN
EVERETT, WA

Stir in the chile pepper and jalapeño pepper juices to really add some sizzle to this salsa.

1 Combine all ingredients in a serving bowl; mix well. Cover with plastic wrap; refrigerate overnight.

Serves 12 to 15

3 15-1/2 oz. cans stewed tomatoes, chopped

8-oz. can tomato sauce

4-oz. can diced green chiles

2-1/4 oz. can black olives, chopped

1 bunch green onions, chopped

2 cloves garlic, chopped

2 T. rice wine vinegar

2 T. olive oil

4-oz. can chopped jalapeño peppers

WASHINGTON WONDERS

If you go to Safeco Field to see the Mariners play baseball, garlic fries are must-have snacks, say many locals.

GAME-DAY DIM SUM

CARLY ST. CLAIR
LYNNWOOD, WA

My husband John and son Greg are learning Chinese together. Adding some Chinese home cooking to your game-day feast will be good eats and good memories! If you don't have any chili oil, you can substitute red pepper flakes.

2 lbs. ground beef
1 T. fresh ginger, peeled and grated
1 T. garlic, minced
1 T. soy sauce
1 T. white wine or chicken broth
1 t. chili oil
3 green onions, chopped
1/2 red onion, diced
1 T. cornstarch
salt and pepper to taste
48 wonton wrappers
Garnish: additional soy sauce for dipping

1 In a bowl, combine all ingredients except wonton wrappers and garnish; mix well. Place one tablespoon beef mixture into the center of each wrapper. Bring corners of wrapper together above beef mixture and twist, sealing edges. Place wontons in a steamer that has been sprayed with non-stick vegetable spray. Steam on high setting for 20 to 30 minutes, until beef mixture is cooked through. Serve with soy sauce for dipping.

Makes 16 servings

GOLDEN CHEESE PUFFS

ROBIN HUMBERSTAD
PROSSER, WA

Add a little more cayenne if you want an appetizer with a kick.

1 Mix the first 5 ingredients together; spread on bread slices. Arrange on ungreased baking sheets; bake at 425 degrees until golden and bubbly, about 15 minutes.

Serves 8 to 12

8-oz. pkg. cream cheese, softened
1/2 c. mayonnaise
2 T. onion, chopped
1/4 c. grated Parmesan Cheese
1/8 t. cayenne pepper
1 loaf sliced party rye or wheat bread

APPLE & BRIE TOASTS

JO ANN
GOOSEBERRY PATCH

These little tidbits of flavor are so showy and easy to make. We make them often!

1 Arrange baguette slices on an ungreased baking sheet; bake at 350 degrees until lightly toasted. Set aside.

2 Mix together brown sugar, walnuts and butter. Top each slice of bread with a cheese slice, an apple slice and 1/2 teaspoon of brown sugar mixture. Bake at 350 degrees until cheese melts,

Makes 2-1/2 dozen, serves 30

1 baguette, cut into 1/4-inch-thick slices
1/4 c. brown sugar, packed
1/4 c. chopped walnuts
3 T. butter, melted
13.2-oz. pkg. Brie cheese, thinly sliced
3 Granny Smith apples and/or Braeburn apples, cored and sliced

HOT PEPPERONI DIP

VICKIE
GOOSEBERRY PATCH

*For a milder version, use banana peppers. Keep lots of toasted
bread sticks or garlic bread on hand for dipping...yum!*

2 c. shredded mozzarella
  cheese
2 c. shredded sharp
  Cheddar cheese
2 c. mayonnaise
1 red onion, chopped
4-oz. can diced green
  chiles, drained
2 to 3 jalapeño peppers
10 to 20 pepperoni slices

1 Combine cheeses, mayonnaise, onion, chiles and
peppers; place in an ungreased 13"x9" baking pan.
Layer pepperoni on top; bake at 350 degrees for
45 minutes.

Serves 10

KITCHEN TIP

To save time, use a food processor
to quickly chop onion and pepper
or purchase them pre-chopped
from your supermarket.

MARINATED OLIVES

PAT GENO
EVERETT, WA

My kids' favorite olive recipe...they request it at all holidays.

1 Combine all ingredients; mix well and place in a covered container. Refrigerate for 2 hours before serving. May be kept refrigerated up to one month.

Makes about 2 cups

2 6-oz. cans whole black olives, drained
1/2 c. olive oil
1/4 c. fresh oregano or basil, chopped
4 cloves garlic, minced
2 T. balsamic vinegar
1 t. red pepper flakes
1/2 t. salt

MAC & CHEESE NUGGETS

LIZ PLOTNICK-SNAY
GOOSEBERRY PATCH

Everyone loves mac & cheese and now they become pick-up snack favorites.

1 Lightly grease mini muffin cups. Sprinkle with 2 tablespoons Parmesan cheese, tapping out excess. Melt butter in a large saucepan over medium heat. Stir in flour; cook for 2 minutes. Whisk in milk until boiling, about 5 minutes. Add Cheddar and American cheeses; remove from heat and stir until smooth. Whisk in egg yolk and paprika; fold in macaroni until well coated.

2 Spoon rounded tablespoons of mixture into prepared tins; sprinkle with remaining Parmesan. Bake at 425 degrees until hot and golden, about 10 minutes. Cool for 5 minutes; carefully transfer to a serving plate.

Makes 4 dozen

1/4 c. grated Parmesan cheese, divided
1-1/2 T. butter
2 T. all-purpose flour
3/4 c. milk
1-1/4 c. shredded Cheddar cheese
1/4 lb. American cheese slices, chopped
1 egg yolk, beaten
1/4 t. paprika
8-oz. pkg. elbow macaroni, cooked

MOM'S BEST MARINADE

LORNA PETERSEN
BURBANK, WA

When we went camping, we always marinated our steak or chicken with this recipe. So easy to follow, just place the meat in a bowl, pierce it slightly with a fork, then top with the marinade. Marinate meat in the refrigerator for 2 hours to 2 days and grill using your favorite recipe.

1/2 c. soy sauce
1/8 t. garlic, minced
2 T. brown sugar, packed
1 t. ground ginger
2 T. vinegar

1 Mix all ingredients together.

Makes about 3/4 cup

STICKY-SWEET CARAMEL APPLES

MELODY TAYNOR
EVERETT, WA

I like to use the smallest apples I can find and make 'em mini... so cute for party favors! You'll be able to make 10 to 12 mini apples with this recipe.

4 to 6 wooden treat sticks
4 to 6 Gala or Jonagold apples
14-oz. pkg. caramels, unwrapped
2 T. milk
Optional: candy sprinkles, chopped nuts, mini candy-coated chocolates

1 Insert sticks into apples; set aside. Combine caramels and milk in a microwave-safe bowl. Microwave, uncovered, for 2 minutes, stirring once. Allow to cool briefly. Roll each apple quickly in caramel, turning to coat. Set apples to dry on lightly greased wax paper. When partially set, roll in toppings, if desired.

Makes 4 to 6

PHIL'S FAMOUS BEAN DIP

JENNIFER ROSE BLAY
PUYALLUP, WA

When I was growing up, my stepdad Phil made this awesome bean dip for all of my birthday parties and our family get-togethers. It was always a big hit! Now I carry on the tradition. I added the jalapeño flavored cheese dip to give it an extra special kick.

1 In a large microwave-safe bowl, combine all ingredients except tortilla chips. Mix well; cover with plastic wrap.

2 Microwave on high setting until all of the cheese is melted, stirring after every minute. Serve warm with tortilla chips.

Serves 8 to 10

16-oz. can refried beans
16-oz. jar favorite salsa
3 c. shredded Cheddar cheese
9-oz. can jalapeño Cheddar cheese dip
tortilla chips

VICKIE'S FAVORITE GUACAMOLE

VICKIE
GOOSEBERRY PATCH

Whenever we have a Mexican-themed potluck here at Gooseberry Patch, I'm requested to bring my guacamole. It's almost foolproof and oh-so-good!

1 Scoop pulp out of avocados into a bowl. Mash to desired consistency with a potato masher. Add remaining ingredients; mix well. Serve with your favorite tortilla chips.

Makes 2 cups

4 avocados, halved and pitted
1 onion, chopped
2 cloves garlic, minced
2 T. lime juice
1/8 t. kosher salt
tortilla chips

REUBEN DIP

LINDA SICKLER
BRUSH PRAIRIE, WA

This is my most-requested appetizer at gatherings and believe me, there are never any leftovers!

1/2 lb. deli corned beef, diced
8-oz. pkg. cream cheese, softened
1 c. shredded Swiss cheese
1 c. sauerkraut, drained
1/2 c. sour cream
1 T. catsup
2 t. spicy brown mustard
rye crackers or sliced party rye bread

1 Stir all ingredients except crackers or bread together in a bowl; spoon into a greased one-quart casserole dish.

2 Bake, uncovered, at 350 degrees for 30 minutes, or until hot and bubbly. Serve warm with bread or crackers.

Serves 6 to 8

WASHINGTON WONDERS

What is boba or bubble tea? It's an extremely popular Asian drink in Seattle, with lots of spots to enjoy it. It's a combination of flavorful tea, chewy tapioca pearls and milk. It's from Taiwan. There are numerous flavors available, including a brown sugar blend.

ROSEMARY-WHITE BEAN DIP

JO ANN
GOOSEBERRY PATCH

Rosemary is one of my favorite herbs, so I always have a couple pots of it growing on my windowsill. A good friend shared this recipe with me, and I just knew I had to try it. So one game day I whipped up a batch, and was it a hit!

1 Combine beans, garlic, rosemary, pepper flakes and broth in a medium slow cooker. Cover and cook on high setting for 3 hours, or until beans are soft and liquid is mostly absorbed. Remove crock and cool.

2 Place cooled bean mixture into a blender; stir in oil and lemon juice. Process until dip reaches desired consistency. Spoon dip into a serving bowl; sprinkle with parsley. Serve with dippers.

Serves 4 to 6

3/4 c. dried white beans
4 cloves garlic, minced
1 T. fresh rosemary, chopped
1 t. red pepper flakes
2 c. vegetable broth
salt to taste
7 T. olive oil
1-1/2 T. lemon juice
1 T. fresh parsley, chopped
assorted dippers such as crackers, toasted baguette slices and cherry tomatoes

SPICY CHEESE DIP

ALYSSA DAVIS
OLYMPIA, WA

I made up this recipe ten years ago for a football party, and it was a hit! I have served it for baby showers, wedding showers, barbecues, birthday parties, goodbye parties, you name it. People request it all the time. It is so yummy.

16-oz. pkg. pasteurized process cheese, cubed

8-oz. pkg. Mexican pasteurized process cheese, cubed

16-oz. pkg. spicy ground pork sausage, browned and drained

1 lb. ground beef, browned and drained

10-3/4 oz. can cream of mushroom soup

16-oz. can chili no beans

2 14-1/2 oz. cans mild or hot diced tomatoes with green chiles

16-oz. jar hot salsa

tortilla chips

1 Combine all ingredients except chips in a 6-quart slow cooker; mix well. Cover and cook on high setting for 4 hours, or until cheese is fully melted.

2 Turn to low setting for serving. Serve with tortilla chips.

Makes 20 to 30 servings

SPINACH-ARTICHOKE DIP

RACHEL ADAMS
FORT LEWIS, WA

I make this delectable dip for special occasions...family & friends rave about its tantalizing taste! Have copies of the recipe on hand, because you're going to need them to hand out.

1 Combine chopped artichokes, spinach and cheeses in a slow cooker; mix well. Stir in garlic and pepper.

2 Cover and cook on high setting for about one to 2 hours, stirring occasionally, until cheeses are melted and dip is smooth. Reduce heat to low setting to keep warm. Serve with pita chips and sliced vegetables for dipping.

Serves 10 to 12

14-oz. can artichoke hearts, drained and chopped
2 bunches fresh spinach, chopped
2 8-oz. pkgs. reduced-fat cream cheese, softened and cubed
2-1/2 c. shredded Monterey Jack cheese
2-1/2 c. shredded mozzarella cheese
3 cloves garlic, minced
1/4 t. pepper
pita chips and assorted sliced vegetables for dipping

KITCHEN TIP

Fresh cloves of garlic always taste great in recipes, but keep a little jar of minced garlic in your fridge in case you run out of fresh! You can use 1/2 teaspoon of garlic from the jar for each clove called for.

CHAPTER FIVE

TIME-FOR-A-TREAT
Desserts

**FROM COAST TO COAST, THERE
IS ALWAYS ROOM FOR DESSERT.
SO SIT BACK AND ENJOY A
LITTLE SWEET TREAT AT THE
END OF YOUR MEAL.**

APPLE BLUSH PIE

KATHERINE BARRETT
BELLEVUE, WA

*This recipe goes back about eighty years in my family. It was
always made with apples from the trees in our yard.*

5 apples, peeled, cored
and sliced

3/4 c. sugar

15-1/4 oz. can crushed
pineapple

1/3 c. red cinnamon
candies

2 T. instant tapioca,
uncooked

3 T. butter, softened

2 9-inch pie crusts

1 In a bowl, combine all ingredients except crusts.
Place one crust in a 9" pie plate; top with apple
mixture. Cut remaining crust into 1/2-inch strips;
form a lattice pattern over filling.

2 Bake at 425 degrees for 10 minutes. Reduce
temperature to 350 degrees and bake an additional
30 minutes. Let cool.

Serves 8

BONUS IDEA

Surprise your chocolate-chip-
cookie-lover friends with a treat
they will never forget! Put a
scoop of ice cream between two
cookies and make an ice-cream
sandwich. Yummy!

APRICOT LAYER BARS

MARILYN ROGERS
PORT TOWNSEND, WA

A classic recipe...one bite and you'll know why!

1 Mix together oats, flour, brown sugar, butter and salt. Press half of the mixture into a greased 8"x8" baking pan.

2 Spread preserves over the top; top with remaining oat mixture. Bake at 350 degrees for 35 minutes. Let cool; cut into squares.

Makes one to 1-1/2 dozen

1-3/4 c. quick-cooking oats, uncooked
1-3/4 c. all-purpose flour
1 c. brown sugar, packed
1 c. butter, softened
1/8 t. salt
12-oz. jar apricot preserves

YUMMY GOLDEN NUGGETS

ROBIN WERNER
BRUSH PRAIRIE, WA

I like to make these tasty no-bake treats for Saint Patrick's Day and wrap them in gold foil to look like lucky coins.

1 Spread one cracker with one to 2 teaspoons of peanut butter. Top with another to form a sandwich. Repeat to make 12 sandwiches.

2 Melt butterscotch chips in the top of a double boiler over medium heat, stirring occasionally until melted and smooth. Dip each sandwich completely into melted butterscotch. Place on parchment paper to cool.

Makes one dozen

24 round buttery crackers
1/2 to 1 c. creamy peanut butter
2 c. butterscotch chips

BEACON HILL COOKIES

JODI HOPKINS
EVERETT, WA

My Great-Grandma Ann was a remarkable woman who lived to be 104. She credited that to her good Swedish genes as well as "never eating anything from a box." These cookies were one of my favorites. After she died, I asked my grandma if she had the recipe...I was so pleased that we found it, in Great-Grandma's handwriting!

1 c. butter, softened
1 c. sugar
2 egg yolks
1 t. vanilla extract
1-1/2 c. all-purpose flour
1/4 t. baking powder
1/8 t. salt
3/4 c. long-cooking oats, uncooked
3/4 c. crispy rice cereal

1 In a large bowl, blend all ingredients. Roll into one-inch balls; arrange on greased baking sheets. Press cookies with a fork, making a criss-cross shape.

2 Bake at 375 degrees for 10 minutes, or until golden.

Makes 3 dozen

BEST CHOCOLATE CHIP COOKIES

SAMANTHA REILLY
GIG HARBOR, WA

This is my family's favorite cookie recipe! We often end up eating at least half of the dough, as it's almost as good that way.

1-1/2 c. butter, softened
1 c. sugar
1 c. brown sugar, packed
3 eggs, beaten
1-1/2 t. vanilla extract
3-1/2 c. all-purpose flour
2 t. baking powder
1-1/2 t. salt
12-oz. pkg. semi-sweet chocolate chips

1 In a large bowl, blend together butter and sugars; stir in eggs and vanilla. In a separate bowl, mix together flour, baking powder and salt. Gradually add flour mixture to butter mixture; mix well. Fold in chocolate chips. Spoon dough by heaping tablespoonfuls onto ungreased baking sheets.

2 Bake at 350 degrees for 10 to 12 minutes for chewy cookies, 12 to 13 minutes for soft cookies or 15 minutes for crunchy cookies. Cool on wire racks.

Makes 2 dozen

CHERRY BERRY CHOCOLATE CAKE

VICKIE
GOOSEBERRY PATCH

Here's a cake that is as beautiful as it is delicious! Use local berries when you can find them. Yum!

1 Blend butter, shortening, sugar and vanilla until fluffy; blend in eggs and set aside. In a separate bowl, combine flour, cocoa, baking powder and salt; add flour mixture alternately with milk to sugar mixture. Stir well.

2 Pour into 2 greased and floured 8" round cake pans. Bake at 350 degrees for 30 to 35 minutes, until a toothpick tests done. Cool and frost cake between layers and on top, putting fresh berries in middle and on top.

Makes 16 servings

1/4 c. butter, softened
1/4 c. shortening
2 c. sugar
1 t. vanilla extract
2 eggs, beaten
1-3/4 c. all-purpose flour
3/4 c. baking cocoa
1 t. baking powder
3/4 t. salt
1-3/4 c. milk
3 c. mixed fresh cherries and berries

1 To butter, add cocoa and powdered sugar alternately with milk. Mix in vanilla; stir until creamy.

FROSTING:
4 T. butter, softened
1/3 c. baking cocoa
2 c. powdered sugar
1/4 c. milk
1 t. vanilla extract

BUTTERSCOTCH SPICE HAND CAKE

FAYE LENGENFELDER
RENTON, WA

I've made this recipe many years for my three boys. This cake is easy to make and you can eat it out of hand...great for snacking!

3-1/2 oz. pkg. cook & serve butterscotch pudding mix
2 c. milk
15-1/4 oz. pkg. spice cake mix
6-oz. pkg. butterscotch chips
1 c. chopped nuts

1 In a large saucepan, combine dry pudding mix and milk; cook according to package directions. Add dry cake mix to hot pudding; stir until well mixed.

2 Pour batter into a 13"x9" baking pan sprayed with non-stick vegetable spray. Sprinkle with butterscotch chips and nuts. Bake at 350 degrees for 30 minutes. Cool; cut into squares.

Serves 12

STRAWBERRY GRATIN

LISA KASTNING
MARYSVILLE, WA

One of my very favorite recipes...it's delicious and so easy. I make it every strawberry season and everyone loves it!

8 c. strawberries, hulled and quartered
1-1/2 c. sour cream
2 T. half-and-half
1/8 t. salt
1/2 c. dark brown sugar, packed
Optional: ice cream, pound cake

1 Place strawberries in an ungreased 13"x 9" baking pan. In a bowl, whisk together sour cream, half-and-half and salt. Spoon mixture evenly over berries. Sprinkle brown sugar over sour cream mixture.

2 Broil until brown sugar has melted and is lightly golden. Serve as is, or spooned over ice cream or slices of pound cake.

Serves 6

CHOCOLATE CHERRY DELIGHTS

MAUREEN ERICKSON
EVERETT, WA

Here's another must-make recipe for Christmas...I got it a few years ago from my sister-in-law. It's a no-bake treat.

1 Mix together all ingredients except chocolate chips and paraffin. Form into one-inch balls; set aside.

2 Melt chocolate chips and paraffin in a double boiler over medium-low heat until smooth. Dip balls into chocolate mixture to coat; let stand on wax paper until set.

Makes about 2-1/2 dozen

1/4 c. butter, melted
2 c. powdered sugar
1/2 c. dried cherries, finely chopped
2/3 c. creamy peanut butter
1 c. chopped walnuts
1 c. sweetened flaked coconut
1/8 t. salt
6-oz. pkg. semi-sweet chocolate chips
3-1/2 T. paraffin, chopped

WASHINGTON WONDERS

Cherries, cherries, cherries! Sample all your favorites from Washington state...Bing, Queen Anne and Rainier.

SPICED APPLESAUCE CAKE

**DESIREE HARRIS
ROSLYN, WA**

I tweaked a recipe to create my own fruit-filled version. I love that the cake is so moist and flavorful, yet uses only a little butter. It just proves that you don't need all that fat to make a great cake! I have sent this to work with my husband at the Fire Department several times and it always gets rave reviews. I don't frost this cake because it is yummy as is.

1/2 c. butter, softened
2 eggs, beaten
1-1/2 c. unsweetened
  natural applesauce
2-1/2 c. all-purpose flour
1-1/4 c. brown sugar,
  packed, or white sugar
3/4 t. baking powder
1-1/2 t. baking soda
1 t. salt
1/2 c. water
1 t. vanilla extract
1-1/2 t. apple pie spice
1 t. cinnamon
1/2 t. ground cardamom
1/2 c. raisins
1/2 c. dried cranberries
1 c. canned pears,
  chopped
1 c. canned peaches,
  chopped

1 In a large bowl, combine butter, eggs and applesauce; beat together until smooth. Add remaining ingredients except fruits; stir until combined. Stir in fruits. Pour into a 13"x9" baking pan coated with non-stick vegetable spray.

2 Bake at 350 degrees for 45 to 50 minutes, until a toothpick inserted in the center tests clean. Cut into squares.

Makes 12 to 15 servings

COLOSSAL ALASKA COOKIES

DWEE BAKER
OAKVILLE, WA

These cookies are made without any flour. This recipe was an Alaskan logging camp special that my mother-in-law Shirley shared with me, so you know it's extra hearty and good.

1 Mix together sugars, eggs and butter in a very large bowl; beat well. Add oats, peanut butter and baking soda; mix well. Fold in remaining ingredients.

2 Place by 1/4 cupfuls 4 inches apart on lightly greased baking sheets; press flat with your hand. Bake at 350 degrees for 10 to 15 minutes. Let cool for 3 minutes on baking sheets; transfer to a wire rack to cool completely.

Makes about 8 dozen

1-1/2 c. sugar

1-1/2 c. brown sugar, packed

4 eggs, beaten

1/2 c. butter, softened

6 c. long-cooking oats, uncooked

18-oz. jar creamy peanut butter

2-1/2 t. baking soda

6-oz. pkg. semi-sweet chocolate chips

6-oz. pkg. peanut butter chips

KITCHEN TIP

Be sure to let your butter soften before beating with sugar so no lumps will form. You'll get perfect results every time!

FROSTED BANANA BARS

DANA ROWAN
SPOKANE, WA

I have been making this recipe for years. It is always requested when we have a work potluck and there are never any leftovers...ever! I have a friend who is an extremely picky eater. This is one of the only desserts she will eat. She started calling it "Frosted Sin" because it is so yummy and decadent. It is easy to make and a great way to use up extra bananas that are sitting around your kitchen.

1/2 c. butter, softened
2 c. sugar
3 eggs, beaten
1-1/2 c. ripe bananas, mashed
1 t. vanilla extract
2 c. all-purpose flour
1 t. baking soda
1/8 t. salt

1 In a large bowl, blend butter and sugar until light and fluffy. Beat in eggs, bananas and vanilla. In a separate bowl, combine flour, baking soda and salt; stir into butter mixture, just until blended. Spread batter in a greased 15"x10" jelly-roll pan.

2 Bake at 350 degrees for 20 to 25 minutes, until a toothpick inserted in the center tests clean. Allow to cool completely; spread with Powdered Sugar Frosting. Cut into bars.

Makes 3 dozen

POWDERED SUGAR FROSTING:

8-oz. pkg. cream cheese, softened
1/2 c. butter, softened
4 c. powdered sugar
2 t. vanilla extract

1 In a large bowl, beat cream cheese and butter until fluffy. Add powdered sugar and vanilla; beat until smooth.

FRUITY POPCORN BARS

MELODY TAYNOR
EVERETT, WA

A perfect pick-me-up on a busy shopping day.

1 Line a 13"x9" baking pan with aluminum foil; spray lightly with non-stick vegetable spray. Toss together popcorn, chocolate chips, cranberries, coconut and almonds in a large bowl; set aside.

2 Melt marshmallows and butter in a saucepan over medium heat; stir until smooth. Pour over popcorn mixture and toss to coat completely; quickly pour into prepared pan. Lay a sheet of wax paper over top and press down firmly. Chill for 30 minutes, or until firm. Lift bars from pan, using foil as handles; peel off foil and wax paper. Slice into bars and chill an additional 30 minutes.

Makes 16

- 3-oz. pkg. microwave popcorn, popped
- 3/4 c. white chocolate chips
- 3/4 c. sweetened dried cranberries
- 1/2 c. sweetened flaked coconut
- 1/2 c. slivered almonds, coarsely chopped
- 10-oz. pkg. marshmallows
- 3 T. butter

GRANDMA'S BUTTER COOKIES

ANETT YEAGER
BATTLE GROUND, WA

Grandma would make these cookies for all the grandkids on Christmas Eve. It was our tradition to eat them after we opened our presents.

1 In a large bowl, combine butter and sugar; stir until creamy. Slowly stir in flour; form dough into a ball. If too soft, add a little more flour. On a floured surface, roll out dough to about 1/4-inch thick. Cut out with cookie cutters; place on ungreased baking sheets.

2 In a small bowl, beat egg white with water; brush over cookies. Add sprinkles, if desired. Bake at 350 degrees for 6 to 7 minutes, until golden. Cool on a wire rack.

Makes 2 dozen

- 1 c. butter, room temperature
- 1/2 c. sugar
- 2 c. all-purpose flour
- 1 egg white
- 1 t. water
- Optional: colored sprinkles

GRANDMA ROSE'S
NEVER-FAIL PIE CRUST

CAREY BENTSON
ELMA, WA

On Thanksgiving, Grandma Rose's house was the place to be. Her pies were the crown jewels on the cooling rack out back, hidden from anyone wanting to take a taste or two. She loved to cook and her pie crusts were the best...always so flaky and good!

1 egg, lightly beaten
2 T. vinegar
5 c. all-purpose flour
3 c. butter-flavored shortening

1 Combine egg and vinegar in a one-cup measuring cup. Add enough cold water to fill the cup; set aside. Add flour to a large bowl; cut in shortening with a pastry blender or 2 knives. Blend together until shortening is well mixed into flour. Add egg mixture; stir well until dough is clumpy but not wet. Add a little more flour if needed.

2 Divide dough into 6 to 7 rounded portions. Use immediately, or wrap well in plastic wrap; refrigerate up to 2 weeks, or freeze up to one year.

Makes 6 to 7 single 9-inch pie crusts

To use: Thaw overnight in refrigerator, if frozen. Roll out on a floured surface, about 1/4-inch thick and 12 inches in diameter. Place in a 9" pie plate. Bake according to your recipe.

BUTTERSCOTCH PIE

CINDY NEEL
GOOSEBERRY PATCH

I made this old-fashioned pie for my dad's birthday...yum! It has a really rich butterscotch flavor. Top each slice with a generous dollop of whipped cream.

1 In a saucepan over medium-low heat, stir together brown sugar and butter until butter melts and sugar dissolves.

2 Cook 2 to 3 minutes longer; remove from heat. In a separate bowl, mix together flour and one cup milk until smooth. Add egg yolks and salt; mix well and stir in remaining milk. Add flour mixture to brown sugar mixture in saucepan.

3 Cook over medium-low heat until thickened, stirring constantly. Remove from heat; stir in vanilla. Spoon filling into crust; chill thoroughly.

Serves 6 to 8

1 c. light brown sugar, packed
1/4 c. butter, softened
1/4 c. all-purpose flour
2 c. whole milk, divided
3 egg yolks, beaten
1/8 t. salt
1/2 t. vanilla extract
9-inch graham cracker crust

GRANDMA'S HERMITS

**GLENDA MITCHELL
DARRINGTON, WA**

*My grandma baked these cookies for me when I was little, back
in the 1950s. I always got to mix the shortening, sugar and eggs
together and help put them on the baking sheet. At the ripe old age
of five years, I really thought I was a great cook! She's gone now,
but the spicy smell of Hermits baking always reminds me of her.*

1 c. shortening
1-1/2 c. sugar
3 eggs, beaten
1/2 t. baking soda
2 t. water
3 c. all-purpose flour
1-1/2 t. salt
1 t. cinnamon
1 t. allspice
1 t. nutmeg
1 t. ground cloves
1-1/2 c. raisins, dried
   cherries or dried
   cranberries
1/2 c. chopped nuts

1 In a large bowl, blend together shortening, sugar
and eggs; set aside. In a cup, dissolve baking soda
in water; add to shortening mixture. In a separate
bowl, sift together flour, salt and spices; add to
shortening mixture and mix well.

2 Fold in raisins or dried fruit and nuts. Drop by
teaspoonfuls onto greased baking sheets. Bake at
350 degrees for 15 to 20 minutes.

Makes about 6 dozen

HUCKLEBUCKS

SHANNON ELLIS
MOUNT VERNON, WA

*Soft chocolate cookies with a marshmallow filling...everybody
I know loves these tasty treats!*

1 In a large bowl, beat together shortening, eggs, cocoa, sugar and 1-1/2 teaspoons vanilla. In a separate bowl, sift together flour, baking powder and 3/4 teaspoon salt. Add 1-1/2 cups milk to cocoa mixture, alternating with dry ingredients. Mix well after each addition until batter is smooth.

2 Drop by tablespoonfuls onto ungreased baking sheets. Bake at 400 degrees for 7 to 8 minutes; cool. Blend together remaining vanilla, salt, milk and other ingredients; spread on one side of a cookie and top with a second cookie. Repeat with remaining cookies.

Makes 2 dozen

3/4 c. shortening
2 eggs, beaten
3/4 c. baking cocoa
1-1/2 c. sugar
3 t. vanilla extract, divided
1-1/2 c. all-purpose flour
1 T. baking powder
3/4 t. plus 1/8 t. salt, divided
1-1/2 c. plus 1 T. milk, divided
3/4 c. butter, softened
2 c. powdered sugar
1 c. marshmallow creme

WASHINGTON WONDERS

Artisnal chocolates are popular,
such as Fran's Smoked Salt Caramels.
Likewise, Chukar Cherries and dried fruits
dipped in chocolate are special treats. They are
dehydrated Northwest cherries with no sugar
or preservatives added. The company is based in
Prosser, Washington.

JOEY'S PEACH DUMP CAKE

TINA HENGEN
CLARKSTON, WA

I taught my very special nephew Joey to make this yummy dessert. He was so proud of himself and deemed it one of the best desserts he's ever had!

2 29-oz. cans sliced peaches, divided
18-1/2 oz. pkg. white cake mix
1/2 c. butter, sliced
1 c. brown sugar, packed
2 t. cinnamon
1 c. chopped nuts

1 Pour one can of peaches with juice into a lightly greased 13"x9" baking pan. Drain the remaining can; add peaches to pan. Sprinkle dry cake mix over the top; dot with butter. Combine brown sugar with cinnamon in a bowl; sprinkle over cake mix. Sprinkle nuts over top. Do not stir.

2 Bake, uncovered, at 350 degrees for one hour, or until bubbly and golden.

Makes 8 to 10 servings

CHOCOLATE-BERRY TRIFLES

MELODY TAYNOR
EVERETT, WA

I've made all kinds of trifles, but this is my first one with chocolate. My sister says it's my best yet!

1 pt. blueberries, divided
1 pt. strawberries, hulled and sliced
1 angel food cake, cubed
1 c. chocolate syrup
12-oz. container frozen whipped topping, thawed

1 In a bowl, crush 1/4 cup blueberries. Stir in remaining blueberries and strawberries. Place several cake cubes in the bottom of 10 clear serving cups or bowls. Top with a layer of berry mixture.

2 Drizzle lightly with chocolate syrup, then top with a layer of whipped topping. Repeat layers until each cup is full, ending with a layer of whipped topping and a light drizzle of chocolate syrup.

Makes 10 servings

GRANDMA MARY'S SHORTBREAD

KERRY MCNEIL
ANACORTES, WA

I received this wonderful recipe 20 years ago from a dear friend who was like a grandmother to me. When my husband and I owned a bakery, we used it every spring to bake pink, yellow and violet frosted tulip cookies by the thousands for our county's annual tulip festival.

1 Combine all ingredients in a medium bowl and knead to form a smooth dough. Roll out on a floured surface to 1/4-inch thick. Cut out with a cookie or biscuit cutter.

1 c. butter, softened
2 c. all-purpose flour
1/2 c. superfine sugar
2 T. cornstarch

2 Transfer to ungreased baking sheets. Bake at 275 degrees for 45 minutes; cool. Frost with Cream Cheese Frosting. Refrigerate until set or ready to serve.

Makes 2-1/2 dozen

1 With an electric mixer on medium speed, beat cream cheese and butter together. Add vanilla and mix well. On low speed, add powdered sugar until mixed. Beat on high speed for one minute. Tint with food coloring, if desired.

CREAM CHEESE FROSTING:

8-oz. pkg. cream cheese, softened
1/2 c. butter, softened
2 t. vanilla extract
16-oz. pkg. powdered sugar
Optional: few drops food coloring

MAPLE SUGAR-WALNUT PIE

JO ANN
GOOSEBERRY PATCH

Luscious...a terrific use for pure maple syrup!

1 c. walnuts, coarsely
  chopped and toasted
9-inch pie crust, chilled
3 eggs, beaten
1 c. maple syrup
1/4 c. butter, melted and
  cooled slightly
2/3 c. light brown sugar,
  packed
1/2 t. vanilla extract
1/8 t. salt

1 Scatter walnuts in crust and set aside. In a bowl, whisk together remaining ingredients; pour into crust over nuts. Set pie plate on a baking sheet.

2 Bake at 425 degrees for 10 minutes. Reduce oven to 350 degrees; bake an additional 25 to 30 minutes, until crust is golden and center is set. Cool slightly on a wire rack before serving.

Serves 8

FAMOUS BLUEBERRY CAKE

MELODY TAYNOR
EVERETT, WA

All my friends love it when I bake this blueberry cake. I get the blueberries at the farmers' market when they are fresh. Yummy!

1 c. butter, softened
2 c. sugar
4 eggs, room
  temperature
1 t. vanilla extract
3 c. all-purpose flour
1 t. baking powder
1/2 t. salt
2 c. blueberries
2 t. lemon zest
Garnish: lemon rind
  curls, raw or coarse
  sugar

1 In a large bowl, beat together butter and sugar. Add eggs, one at a time, beating well after each addition. Beat until fluffy and add vanilla. In a separate bowl, mix together flour, baking powder and salt. Set aside one cup of flour mixture. Add remaining flour mixture to butter mixture and beat well. Dredge berries and lemon zest in reserved flour mixture. Gently fold berry mixture into batter. Spoon into a greased and floured 10" tube pan. Sprinkle raw or coarse sugar on top.

2 Bake at 350 degrees for 1-1/4 hours, or until a cake tester inserted near the center comes out clean.

Makes 24 servings

MOM'S BAKED APPLES

MELODY TAYNOR
EVERETT, WA

A comforting chilly-weather dessert or a luscious side for roast pork.

1 Partially core apples from the top; set aside. In a small bowl, mix brown sugar, cinnamon, raisins and walnuts, if using; spoon mixture into apples. Place apples right-side up in a slow cooker; dot with butter. Pour apple juice around apples.

2 Cover and cook on low setting for 5 hours, or on high setting for 2-1/2 hours, until apples are tender. With a large spoon, transfer apples to small bowls. Top with some of the juice mixture over apples; serve warm.

Makes 4 servings

4 Granny Smith apples

1/4 c. brown sugar, packed

1/2 t. cinnamon

1/3 c. golden raisins

Optional: 1/3 c. chopped walnuts

1 T. butter, diced

1/2 c. apple juice

ZUCCHINI BROWNIES

VICKI NELSON
PUYALLUP, WA

My mother gave me this recipe years ago after I married and started growing a garden. Like everyone else, I was always looking for ways to use up zucchini.

1 In a bowl, stir together flour, salt, cocoa and baking soda. Mix in sugar, oil, egg and zucchini. Spread into a lightly greased 15"x10" jelly-roll pan.

2 Bake at 350 degrees for 20 minutes. Let cool; garnish as desired. Cut into squares.

Makes about 1-1/2 dozen

2 c. all-purpose flour

1 t. salt

1/3 c. baking cocoa

1-1/2 t. baking soda

1-1/4 c. sugar

1/2 c. oil

1 egg, beaten

2 c. zucchini, grated

Garnish: chocolate frosting or powdered sugar

MOM'S PISTACHIO DESSERT

**AUTUMN BOCK
FIFE, WA**

This is a yummy make-ahead dessert. I always looked forward to this dessert when my mom made it...now I make it, and my husband raves about how good it is!

1 c. all-purpose flour
1/2 c. butter, softened
1/2 c. chopped walnuts
8-oz. pkg. cream cheese, softened
1 c. powdered sugar
8-oz. container frozen whipped topping, thawed and divided
2 3.4-oz. pkg's. pistachio pudding mix
3 c. milk
1/2 c. slivered almonds

1 Combine flour, butter and walnuts; mix well and spread in an greased 13"x9" baking pan.

2 Bake at 325 degrees for 15 minutes; let cool.

3 Combine cream cheese, powdered sugar and one cup whipped topping; blend well and spread on top of cooled crust.

4 Combine pudding mixes and milk. Mix as package directs; spread pudding over cream cheese layer. Frost with remaining whipped topping; sprinkle with almonds. Chill until serving time.

Makes 12 servings

NO-BAKE ORANGE BALLS

SAMANTHA REILLY
GIG HARBOR, WA

*This recipe has been enjoyed by four generations of my family.
It is a bit of a mess to make, but kids love to make it and they
taste so good that the clean-up is worth it. We used to make
them every year for my grandpa & grandma as well as my great-
grandpa & great-grandma. Now that they have passed on, this
recipe always makes me think of them. Happy memories!*

1 Place a wire rack over a length of wax paper; set
aside. In a large bowl, combine vanilla wafer crumbs
and powdered sugar. Stir in melted butter and
orange juice; set aside.

2 Pour condensed milk into a shallow dish.
Pour coconut into another shallow dish. Form
crumb mixture into walnut-size balls. Dip balls
into condensed milk, coating on all sides; dip into
coconut, coating on all sides. Place balls on a wire
rack to dry. When dry, store in an airtight container
up to 1-1/2 weeks; keep covered.

Makes 4 to 5 dozen

12-oz. pkg. vanilla
  wafers, crushed
16-oz. pkg. powdered
  sugar, sifted
1/2 c. butter, melted
6-oz. can frozen orange
  juice concentrate,
  thawed
14-oz. can sweetened
  condensed milk
7-oz. pkg. shredded
  coconut

PEANUT BUTTER BALLS

KATHLEEN ELVERSTON
FEDERAL WAY, WA

This is a recipe my mom has been making for most holidays and special occasions I can remember. It is so good you can't stop at having only one piece! I use a nut grinder to make the crumbs.

2 c. graham crackers, finely crushed

16-oz. pkg. powdered sugar

1 c. butter, room temperature

3/4 c. creamy peanut butter

1 c. sweetened flaked coconut

1 c. ground walnuts

1 t. vanilla extract

1 Combine all ingredients in a large bowl. Mix well; form into one-inch balls. Set balls on a wax paper-lined baking sheet; refrigerate until firm. Using a toothpick, dip each ball into Chocolate Coating, covering well.

2 Return balls to baking sheet; refrigerate until coating has hardened. Store in a sealed container in the refrigerator.

Makes 2 to 3 dozen

CHOCOLATE COATING:

2 12-oz. pkg's. semi-sweet chocolate chips

1/2 bar paraffin, chopped

1 Combine ingredients in a double boiler; melt and stir until smooth.

PUMPKIN FACE COOKIE PIZZA

SYLVIA JACOBUS
KENT, WA

I've been making this fun dessert ever year since my kids were little. On Halloween they looked forward to this more than anything else. Now, many years later, I'm doing the same thing for the grandkids. They love it too! It's easy to do. And don't worry what to do with leftover candies...I've never had any!

1 Prepare brownie mix according to package directions given for a 13"x9" baking pan. Spread batter evenly on a greased and floured 12" pizza pan.

2 Bake as directed, watching carefully as less time may be needed. Cool completely. Tint frosting with a few drops of food coloring, if desired. Spread frosting evenly over brownie. Use candies to make your favorite Jack-o'-Lantern face. Cut into wedges or squares.

Makes 12 to 16

- 18-oz. pkg. brownie mix
- 16-oz. container vanilla or cream cheese frosting
- Optional: orange food coloring
- 8-oz. pkg. candy-coated chocolates

WASHINGTON WONDERS

Aplets and Cotlets, popular Northwest delicacy of sweet candy treats, are great for snacking and for gifts. Aplets are made from crisp Washington apples and walnuts. Cotlets are made from apricots ("cots") and walnuts for a tangy taste. The Liberty Orchards confections have been made since 1920.

QUICK LUNCHBOX CAKE

**JUDY FINGERSON
AUBURN, WA**

My mother made this when we were kids in the 50s. It's not messy and easy to handle. It really does go well in a lunchbox!

2-1/4 c. all-purpose flour
2 t. baking soda
1 t. salt
1 c. brown sugar, packed
2 eggs, beaten
1/4 c. butter, softened
1 c. fruit cocktail, drained
1/2 c. semi-sweet chocolate chips
1/2 c. chopped nuts

1 Combine all ingredients except chocolate chips and nuts. Blend well with an electric hand mixer on low speed.

2 Pour batter into a greased and floured 13"x9" baking pan. Sprinkle chips and nuts over batter. Bake at 350 degrees for 35 to 40 minutes. Cool and cut into squares.

Makes 16 servings

S'MORE BARS

**JO ANN
GOOSEBERRY PATCH**

All the campfire flavor of s'mores…enjoy them anytime!

8 to 10 whole graham crackers
20-oz. pkg. brownie mix
2 c. mini marshmallows
1 c. semi-sweet chocolate chips
2/3 c. chopped pecans

1 Arrange graham crackers in a single layer in a greased 13"x9" baking pan; set aside. Prepare brownie mix according to package directions; spread carefully over graham crackers.

2 Bake at 350 degrees for 25 to 30 minutes. Sprinkle marshmallows, chocolate chips and pecans over brownie layer; bake for an additional 5 minutes or until golden. Cut into bars when cool.

Makes 2 dozen

RUSTIC PEAR TART

MELODY TAYNOR
EVERETT, WA

Simple to make, this recipe can make one large or many bite-size tarts.

1 Mix one cup flour, one teaspoon sugar, baking powder and salt. Cut in 1/4 cup butter until mixture resembles coarse meal. Add sour cream; stir with a fork until very crumbly. Cover and chill for 30 minutes.

2 Combine pears and lemon juice, 1/4 cup sugar and vanilla; toss to coat. On a lightly floured surface, roll out dough to a 14-inch circle; place on an ungreased baking sheet. Mix remaining flour and sugar; sprinkle evenly over dough.

3 Arrange pear slices on top. Moisten dough edges with water; fold in edges 2 inches over pears. Dot with remaining butter. Bake at 400 degrees for 40 minutes, or until crust is golden. Cool 15 minutes; dust with powdered sugar.

Serves 6 to 8

1 c. plus 2 T. all-purpose flour, divided

1/4 c. plus 4 t. sugar, divided

1/4 t. baking powder

1/4 t. salt

1/4 c. plus 1 t. chilled butter, diced and divided

3 T. sour cream

1-1/2 lbs. pears, peeled, cored and sliced

1 T. lemon juice

1/2 t. vanilla extract

Garnish: powdered sugar

CHEDDAR CRUMBLE APPLE PIE

JO ANN
GOOSEBERRY PATCH

*Warm apple pie is delicious topped with a slice of Cheddar
cheese. This clever recipe bakes the Cheddar right into the pie.
Give it a try!*

1/2 c. sugar

1/2 c. brown sugar,
packed

3/4 t. cinnamon

11-oz. pkg. pie crust mix,
divided

3 T. chilled butter

2 c. shredded sharp
Cheddar cheese,
divided

2 to 2-1/2 T. water

3 lbs. tart apples, peeled,
cored and sliced

1 T. all-purpose flour

sugar and nutmeg to
taste

Optional: vanilla ice
cream

1 In a large bowl, combine sugars, cinnamon and
half of dry pie crust mix. Cut in butter with a fork until
crumbly; set aside. In a separate bowl, combine
remaining pie crust mix and one cup cheese. Stir in
water until dough forms.

2 Roll out dough on a floured surface; line a 9" pie
plate. In a separate bowl, toss apples with flour; add
sugar and nutmeg to taste.

3 Spoon apples into pie crust; top with half of sugar
mixture, remaining cheese and remaining sugar
mixture. Bake at 375 degrees for about 40 minutes,
or until topping is golden and apples are tender.
Serve warm, topped with ice cream if desired.

Makes 6 to 8 servings

SLOW-COOKER TAPIOCA PUDDING

LEISHA HOWARD
SEATTLE, WA

When I was a child, my mom and I often made stovetop tapioca pudding and I was the stirrer. Even though both my arms would get tired, I loved helping her in the kitchen. Now that I'm older, I've mastered this slow-cooker recipe...it's just as yummy!

1 Add milk, tapioca and sugar to a slow cooker; stir gently. Cover and cook on high setting for 3 hours.

2 In a bowl, mix together eggs, extracts and 2 spoonfuls of hot milk mixture from slow cooker. Slowly stir mixture into slow cooker.

3 Cover and cook on high setting for an additional 20 minutes. Chill overnight. Garnish as desired.

Serves 10 to 12

8 c. milk

1 c. small pearl tapioca, uncooked

1 to 1-1/2 c. sugar

4 eggs, beaten

1 t. vanilla extract

1/2 t. almond extract

Garnish: whipped cream, sliced fresh fruit

INDEX